THE I's HAVE IT
Reflections on Introversion in Student Affairs

2nd Edition

by Amma Marfo

Copyright 2014 Amma Marfo. All rights reserved.

Amma Marfo, Author

Sue Caulfield, Illustrator

TABLE OF CONTENTS

Updates for the Second Edition	3
Introduction	4
Disclaimer	26
Chapter One: The Myth of Solitude	32
Chapter Two: The Myth of Silence	53
Chapter Three: The Myth of Separation	84
Chapter Four: Behind the Mask	100
Chapter Five: The Introverted Interviewee	128
Chapter Six: The Introverted Employee	146
Chapter Seven: The Introverted Graduate Student	172
Chapter Eight: The Introverted Conferencegoer	186
Chapter Nine: The Introverted Educator	207
Chapter Ten: The Introverted Manager	224
Conclusion	240
Acknowledgements	244
On the Shoulders of Giants: References and Guides for Further Reading	248

UPDATES FOR THE SECOND EDITION

The first edition of this book exceeded even my wildest expectations, but as I continued research on this topic, while talking to professionals and students that benefitted from the content, I realized that I wanted there to be more actionable pieces for those *doing* the work that our field calls for.

To that end, this edition features "INsights" at the end of each chapter that will summarize its contents, and provide a few tips that you can place in your introvert survival kit.

Additionally, read on after the References for a bonus guide for interviewing the introvert. Our best chance to improve our ability to reach all students, is to create processes that allow us to bring introverts into our organizations. This guide will help you advance that goal from the start- in the hiring process.

I truly hope you enjoy the added means by which to operationalize the knowledge first shared in this format almost a year ago; may it serve you well as you go out and try to make your mark in our loud world!

Amma Marfo
December 2014

INTRODUCTION

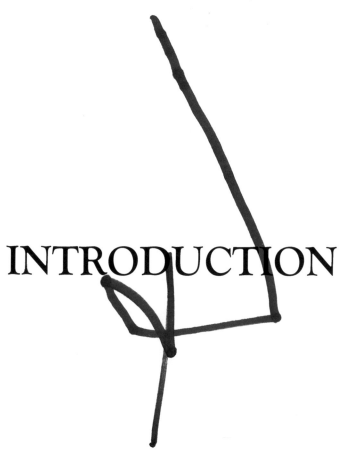

As I write these words, America is in the throes of a quiet revolution.

While the meek are far from inheriting the Earth, they do have a voice as they never have. And the introverted among us owe that renewed voice to writer and former lawyer Susan Cain. Her seminal 2012 book on introversion, *Quiet: The Power of Introverts in a World That Can't Stop Talking*, has given so many introverts a way to understand themselves, and a vehicle to allow others to understand them. She was not the first to write about the "quieter" members of the population, but her book has inexplicably, yet entirely understandably, started an important conversation about where introverts fit in the Western world. Her in-depth and painstaking analysis of the introverted mind broke new ground and has inspired many, myself included.

You may be wondering, if there are so many books already out on the topic of introversion, why write one specifically for student affairs? I noticed, first as a student, then as a graduate student, and even into the early stages of my professional career, there were times when no one knew what to do with me. Clearly motivated and good with students, I also had moments of needing isolation, yearning for solitude in a sea of "open doors". After *Quiet*, and more public knowledge of introversion reached the student affairs world, a funny thing happened. A field typically characterized by boundless energy and effortless gregariousness started to show signs of differentiation. Slowly at first, but then more and more quickly, introverts in this field used their voices purposefully and powerfully to speak up.

They stopped hiding, stopped pretending. As in society, it appeared that far more of us were introverts than previously felt comfortable sharing.

And yet, for all the freedom afforded to introverts to come out of their proverbial hiding, it's still not easy to carry the banner of introversion. There are countless misconceptions circulating about the introverted mind. We're assumed to be aloof, awkward, and antisocial. Interviewers and supervisees assume us to be inattentive and secretive. Our extroverted counterparts remain convinced that if we "put ourselves out there", our nature can be changed. In reality, these myths are easily explained when given the venue and the time (more on that later) to do so.

For those who know me, it may sound crazy to think of a time when I ever fought for my stead as an extrovert. But I did, and it wasn't too long ago. In the Continuing Education course catalog at the University of South Florida, there is a course called "Understanding Yourself and Others: One Key to Effective Leadership and Supervision." As a young college graduate in a new role, I saw value in this idea. I had recently begun supervising student assistants and wanted to be at my best in working with them. I eagerly signed up, and shortly after made the trek to campus for my first class. It was in that first three-hour session that I first started to understand that the effective management of personalities around you is essential to success. After three years as a student leader in college, this was when that essential detail was divulged.

It was during that first class that we took the Myers Briggs Type Indicator, a typology inventory that I vaguely recalled having taken before. I had little memory or understanding of what my results were, so I was excited to take it again and see if my results held. They did, with one key difference. This time around, the test told me I was an introvert.

"I'm not sure this is right," I challenged when asked if we felt our results were correct. "I usually come up as an E!" And it was true. Prior versions of the test had placed me solidly in the land of extroverts. Undeterred by my assertion that the test was wrong, our instructor challenged me. "Are you territorial?" I certainly am. Ask anyone who's borrowed a DVD from me, and then tried to put it back on the shelf without instruction. "How do you feel when you go to parties?" Sometimes the thought of *having* to go to a party exhausts me. There were other telltale signs: my ability to read for long periods without needing to talk to anyone, the ineffectiveness of childhood punishments that called for isolation, my childhood interest in writing and expressing my frustrations through writing.

So why the inconsistency? Why was I so convinced I was an E? In my mind, I couldn't be an 'I'! I didn't hate people; I had a wide circle of friends! I wasn't shy, in middle school I competed in forensic competitions!

As you can probably see, I fell victim to many of the false attributions that come with defining introversion. William Pannapacker saw this very same false attribution when working with his students on issues of introversion and extroversion. After a large percentage of his class revealed itself to be extroverted, he challenged them on their understanding and assumptions of introversion. He found that given the stigma surrounding some of the MBTI's phrasing skews many toward extroversion in its tests. After all, in college, who wants to admit openly that they'd rather be at home than at a party? Who likes the idea of divulging that having a few friends is preferable to having many? In a world where worth is often calculated by one's number of Facebook friends, Twitter followers, or comments on a posted photograph, extroversion is seen as the key to success. This world leaves little leeway for those who communicate differently, who prefer their social circles small, and who speak intentionally.

While this class was not the first time I was made aware of introversion, it was the first time I was helped to *understand* it. Up to this point, I viewed introversion as a stigmatic condition, and no one- no advisors, leadership educators, or professors- advised me to the contrary. This class helped me to realize the good points of introversion, the parts that might be helpful in a group setting. I learned that my natural tendency to listen could make me good at synthesis where others struggled. I learned that my love of writing would prove valuable when summarizing my thoughts. And I learned that being an introvert wasn't synonymous with all I thought it was: shyness, powerlessness, or weakness.

I credit this class with planting a seed of desire to

help students to understand their temperament and that of those around them. That seed was allowed to blossom considerably in my graduate school years (we'll talk about that more later on).

The goal of this book is to delve more deeply into three common strategies introverts use to live in a vocation and a world largely dominated by extroverts. The first section will serve to *demystify* the mind and mannerisms of introversion. Introverts are treated as a minority in society, and operation within a "deficit model" leads to a lot of misunderstanding. By demystifying the introverted way of life, I hope to shine a light on why we are as we are, and what that looks like as we work. The second section will address ways in which we *mask* our true nature. Because temperament is an "invisible" minority, many introverts go through life largely undetected for their true nature. They opt to behave in the manner of the majority; I will address here what that looks like, and what the effects of that strategy can be. The final section of the book will discuss what strategies student affairs professionals have found to *manage* life as introverts in a field and society that doesn't always make that easy. Contrary to popular belief, introverts don't have to operate as extroverts to succeed; this last chapter will provide some guidance on how to be an authentic introvert.

This book is far from a solitary endeavor- I have gathered the insight and advice of many colleagues and friends, fellow introverts. However, this volume will add a factor left largely unaddressed by Susan Cain's work- the voices of extroverts. The perception and opinion of our extroverted counterparts can be of value, and so their perspective has been requested in illuminating the place of introverts in society. I hope that by the conclusion of this book, you the reader will have a greater understanding of what introversion is, how it is perceived, and what the introvert experience can be.

Who is this book for, you may ask?

The Introvert Seeking Understanding
So you may have just learned that you are introverted, or may be wondering if you are an introvert. Welcome. In this book, I hope to place you among friends. This book will give you more insight into how your brain works, what it means

for your behavior, how you might hide your true colors, and how to move from a place of hiding to a place of empowerment. The book will conclude with some strategies for adjusting your behaviors and habits to your workplace. Introverts can be successful within the extrovert ideal; it's just a matter of knowing oneself and learning how to be authentically quiet amidst the whirlwind of the world.

It is also worth noting that bookish introverts tend to hand people books as a way of dispensing advice. For me, the precise book in question (for introverts in student affairs) didn't yet exist, so I'm writing it. If you like it, please feel free to say, "I have something you should read" and pass it along. If just one person can do that, my job will be complete. Speaking of which...

The Extrovert Seeking Understanding
Between the conversations with the extroverts in my own life, and the testimony collected for this book, my suspicions about the mysterious nature attributed to introverts have been confirmed. I'd like to think that this book could help dispel some of the mystery surrounding your introverted friends

and colleagues. The sections on masking introversion may help you identify situations in which your introverted counterparts may need a break to decompress; take note of the behaviors discussed here and look out for them at times of high stimulation. Even for extroverts, the world is becoming too much. Mobile technology means a need to be contacted at all times, 24 hour news cycle, no time to slow down. Introversion is being embraced now because ALL need to embrace their introverted side. Even the most gregarious people need to slow down sometimes. This book will hopefully help those people too.

As the book moves into the management section, you'll learn about how introverts can best utilize their gifts and tendencies to survive and thrive in an extroverted world. Your knowledge of these strategies can help you advocate for a workplace where all employees, regardless of temperament, can do their best work. This needed advocacy can be particularly helpful for one group in particular...

The Extrovert Supervising an Introvert
Of all the factors can contribute to the success of an employee, a good relationship with a supervisor is

near the top of the list. Part of a good relationship between a supervisor and his or her supervisee is an understanding of what is needed for success. In the case of many introverts, there is an urgent need to adjust for temperament. Extroverted supervisors in particular need to be aware, if sensitive, to this need and how it can be accommodated. Introverts don't need to be coddled or protected from the realities of a workplace, but they do need to be understood. It is my hope that the discussions in this book about the driving forces and manifestations of introversion will start a dialogue in the office that leads to that understanding.

No matter how you came to read this book, I hope to offer you a little something in the vein of Sophia Dembling, author of *The Introvert's Way*, who stated beautifully and with just a little kick (the way I love to write):

> Like tourists managing a foreign language, many extroverts are trying to communicate with us but just don't know the language. No need to be Parisian about it and roll your eyes if the effort was well intended. If a question is posed, just answer pleasantly,

with a little explanation.

Whether you're a foreigner to the world of introversion, or are new to the culture and are still learning the language, I am hoping this book serves as a pleasant little explanation and welcome to our culture. Despite what you've heard, we're happy to have you.

For so many, an understanding of our nature that comes with a "diagnosis" of introversion can feel like a tremendous weight has been lifted from the shoulders. After worrying that our nature was abnormal, it is a relief to understand ourselves. "This is who I am," you may rush to proclaim. "I'm not weird or antisocial or broken, I'm introverted!" That sense of understanding is empowering, liberating, even life-changing.

What it should not be, however, is an excuse. One of the more insightful contributions for this story came from Ryan; an extrovert concerned that advocacy for introversion was turning into a crutch. Ryan is a self-proclaimed "atypical" extrovert, and framed his response to my question around his experience with a popular graphic circulating the

Web, "How to Care for Introverts":

> I have to give you people advanced notice of things? I can't interrupt you? What if what you're saying is just ripe for interruption? It seems almost as though the introverts who made this sign (and those who endorse it) are asking to be handled with kid gloves, because even the slightest tinge of embarrassment will cause them to crumble. The extravert one isn't any better. Publically compliment them and make gestures of affection? I'll pass (both for giving and receiving). It's like they're asking to treat these people like rock stars and be their groupies, because any indication that they aren't the best at being special would cause a downward spiral. Clearly, both of these messages are a little extreme, and probably inaccurate for 90% of the population of both groups.

He goes on to make an important point, one that I hope to return to again and again over the course of this book (emphasis added):

> We are called to do what we are called to do,

and 9 times out of 10, we do that very well. And one of the best ways that we do what we're called to do, despite our apparent incompatibility to do so, is by being adaptable. You have to know that the career path you've chosen isn't going to change to fit your needs, so you have to change to fit its.

As you may have guessed from how this book is structured, I will not be asking you to change your nature to cater to the whims of a field, and indeed a world, that doesn't always understand or embrace introversion. I'm not going to accept that the best way to deal with this discrepancy is to (a) make excuses, or (b) change your proverbial stripes. Rather, I wish to offer a deeper understanding of what introversion truly is (and equally importantly, what it is not), show you what hiding it truly is (and again, what it is not), and - what is in my estimation the most important part - how to unapologetically exist in our environment while being your most authentic self. One of the many rules in the mythical Wedding Crashing Guide in the 2005 film of the same name is one you would do well to follow as you join me on this journey. *Rule #76: No excuses, play like a champion.* Here, champion will have two meanings. You'll become a champion in that you'll be doing your best work because you'll know what conditions you need to be successful. But you'll also become a champion for yourself and the other introverts around you, demonstrating to how best be yourself at work.

Introverts and Student Affairs

> *I have come to realize that my death marches in these days were not vocational per se, but were primarily temperamental. Even before I began pastoral ministry, I was convinced that my personality excluded me from it. There was no room in ministry for someone of my disposition, or so I thought.*

As with so many passages in Adam McHugh's book *Introverts in the Church*, the phrase "pastoral ministry" could have easily been replaced with "student affairs," and its meaning would remain intact. For many of us, our first thoughts of student affairs conjure visions of the more "out front" functional areas- new student orientation, residence life, admissions, leadership programs, or my own area of student activities. And I'm sure many in these roles have had friends, family, or acquaintances respond, after hearing about our work, "*Well, that sounds like fun!*" I would never refute the claim that my work is fun, for I am thankful for the repeated opportunity to profoundly enjoy my work. But what such a statement ignores is that for some, this work is deeply, personally, and fundamentally difficult.

When I speak of this work being difficult, I refer less to the substance of our job descriptions or the duties we are (and aren't!) assigned. I speak more in regards to how our natural constitution and temperament informs the way we do our work. Even in less visible or stereotypically "student affairs-y" areas such as academic or career advising, counseling, or even the registrar's office, introverts can find challenge in the everyday design of this work. From expectations of boundless energetic visibility, to effortless interactions with strangers, some of our most basic job requirements conflict with our equally basic temperamental preferences. And yet, we do it. We enter the field in high numbers. Dr. Debra Sanborn conducted an informal study in 2013 and found that while the most common Myers-Briggs type of student affairs professionals surveyed was the fairly common ENFJ (marked extroverts), the second most common was INFJ (marked introverts), and at an overall rate far higher than many of us would have originally thought. Some may wonder, "How do you account for the high number of introverts in a line of work that seems to fight their nature?"

The answer is simple: *it doesn't.*

Marti Laney says of introvert career choice, "Introverts predominate in fields such as science, architecture, *education*, computer science, solo sports, psychology, the visual, literary and dramatic arts, and ~ believe it or not ~ the military. This is due to their excellent ability to focus and their willingness to explore topics in depth." Indeed, in a line of work that incorporates some form of chaos into nearly all of its functional areas, these skills are (or should be) much appreciated. But Laney puts it simply elsewhere in her writings: "introverts come into the limelight because of their quest for work that has meaning, an unusual talent, or extraordinary circumstances." While I would hesitate to call our work "the limelight", I would say that entry into the field of student affairs does come about for one or more of these reasons. Some come to it to help develop students into well adjusted and well educated adults. Some were singled out for their gifts with people, logistics, or data. And still others were drawn to this work after their own wonderful experience in higher education, and felt called to create a similar experience for others. Whatever the reason, or whatever your temperament, here we all are. The motivations to pursue this work are common, but the approaches to the work and needs to do it successfully differ widely, as does the ease with which it is undertaken.

In Praise Of The Extrovert

The goals I have for this book are to help people, introverts and extroverts alike, understand why this work is difficult for introverts, understand the ways in which we may choose to deal with these difficulties, and offer strategies on how to do this work with temperament-based needs in mind. What's more, it will hopefully help you understand what elements of extroversion make asserting these needs to essential.

I want to close this section with a portion of a blog I wrote in April of 2013 titled "In Praise of the Extrovert". While this book is designed to assist and affirm introverts, I have never wanted that championing to diminish the value or the cause of the extrovert. We are not nemeses or even enemies. We are two ends of a spectrum, with rich blends of our two tendencies in between. So whether you're an extrovert reading this book, or an introvert frustrated with the ways of extroverts, know that I see the merits of all temperaments.

> Do I wish to champion the cause of introverts? Absolutely. I wouldn't be so reverent of the work that Susan Cain has done, or devote my time to writing my own book on the subject, if I didn't think that their nature didn't need to be highlighted. However, I think the understanding of the introvert shouldn't need to be paired with the demonization of the extrovert. To crack a joke often used in other circles, "Some of my best friends are extroverts!"
> So know that even though we are different, and even though we may have a hard time understanding each other, I want to sing the

praises of the extroverted. I salute you. Here are a few reasons why:

Extroverts are includers. So many horror stories around introversion are centered around a more extroverted individual trying to get him to do something they're not always comfortable with. Examples include going to parties where he may not know someone, pulling her out on a dance floor, or encouraging them to stay the extra hour at a networking event when she's already tired. However, think about what that really means. It's not the sordid plot of someone trying to pry a friend from his or her comfort zone. Rather, it's a natural tendency to want to create connections between people. Those energized by outward stimulation like to gather their friends and family around them, and to be pushed into a raucous situation means they appreciate and want your company. So feel uncomfortable if you must, but also feel loved!

Extroverts prompt action. I can't speak for all introverts, but I will say that decision-making and determining a course of action takes me a long time. As a result of that, new initiatives or changes to old ones are hard for me to make. Not because I can't make the change, but I'm insistent upon having all the details in place before I get them executed. The beauty of extroverts in a world that moves as quickly as ours is that they move at a similar speed. They can make a decision and commit to all it involves fairly quickly. And that sort of quick decisiveness is something I really value in my more extroverted counterparts.

Extroverts can be quiet too! When I stopped by my director's office yesterday, he happened to be talking about introversion and extroversion with a pair of our students. He asked me to guess if one of them was introverted and extroverted (it's not a party trick, but occasionally gets treated as such), and I ended up being correct. The other student in the office mentioned that he was extroverted, but was also quiet.
I appreciated him for saying this, because we sometimes forget. Just as not all introverts are

shy or quiet, not all extroverts are loud and rambunctious. Introversion and extroversion live on opposite sides of a spectrum, not opposing sides of a coin. There is grey all over the place, and we all live in it.
So even as I continue to champion the cause of introverts, I still have kind words for my extroverted friends. Don't let Forbes Magazine bring you down...your skills and tendencies are still valued!

So as you move forward through this volume, please note that the regard that I hold for extroverts is high. But we could all stand to learn a little more about introversion and how it looks in our field, so on we go.

DISCLAIMER

As a grammar enthusiast and overall appreciator of the written word, I am always conscious of the need to use common terms when having a conversation. After all, working from different definitions of the same word can lead to trouble or needless misunderstanding. So here, before we get rolling, I want to explain some of the terms that will surface over the course of this book.

When I speak or write about introversion, I do so in the most Jungian of terms. As you may or may not know, the origin of the terms "introvert" (or "intravert", as Jung originally wrote it- fear not, both spellings are correct!) and "extrovert" arose from Jung's 1921 work, *Psychological Types*. This book informed the structure of several other interpretations of temperament, most notably the Myers-Briggs Type Indicator and the Big Five Theory of Personality. Among the many definitions that exist for these terms of temperament, I like Jung's the best for its inclusivity. He describes introversion and extroversion as dominant and auxiliary functions for us all. To put it another way: **we all have elements of both!** Even the most extroverted of people have times when they take on more introverted traits; similarly, introverted individuals have their more extroverted moments. No one is purely one or the other. By introducing the concept of dominant and auxiliary functions, Jung introduces the idea that one way of being is simply easier or more natural to summon in our everyday lives.

I have a tremendous amount of respect for the two inventories I mentioned a moment ago, the Myers-

Briggs Type Indicator and the Big Five Theory of Personality. I have used, and continue to use them, when working with students and professionals alike when helping groups learn about themselves and each other. However, there are very specific reasons that I opted to not adopt the definitions of introversion on which they operate. In the interest of transparency and clarity, I'd like to explain why before we move forward. Cool? Cool.

The PROB with the MBTI

As personality inventories go, the MBTI is among the most ubiquitous in the Western world. Translated into dozens of languages and utilized in myriad industries, it has quite the reputation for providing "a-ha" moments for inventory subjects. However, in its many years and nearly as many reimaginings, it has taken on a life of its own.

Ordinarily, such a common understanding of a concept wouldn't be problematic. But, for all of its assertions of assessing subjects on four spectrums of type, its popular understanding differs considerably. That is to say, a series of metrics that should be viewed as continuous have instead come to be seen as dichotomous. Most notably, people see themselves as one side of a two sided coin: they are *either* introverted *or* extroverted, *either* thinking *or* feeling, and so on. Isabel Myers and Katherine Briggs didn't intend for the test to take on this life, but years of the instrument's administration have muddled its original intent.

By using a metric that differs from the MBTI, it allows all to leave behind the assumptions of the well-known instrument, in favor of a common and less bifurcated definition of the terms at hand.

The One Problem With the Big Five

The Big Five Inventory is another common personality instrument that purportedly can measure Extroversion. Measured on a scale of one to five, one's temperament can be measured on this scale, as well as one's levels of Agreeableness, Conscientiousness, Neuroticism, and Openness to Experience. It could be noted that high scores on each of these scales indicate high levels of the suggested trait. Conversely, low scores indicate a lack of that trait. Therefore, a low number on the Extroversion scale indicates a lack of extroversion.

What does that mean? According to the setup of the Big Five, introversion is essentially defined as *a lack of extroversion*. And in my estimation, this is a misunderstanding of what introversion is. Introversion isn't an inability or lack of interest in the hallmarks of extroversion. Rather, it is a whole other set of competencies and interests that results in behavior that seems to oppose those of the extrovert.

Again, by reinforcing Jung's use of dominant and auxiliary functions, neither introversion nor extroversion are viewed as the superior choice; they are instead two options that one can exercise with ease in daily interactions. Dominance of one over the other is determined by which is easier and more natural, not by which one is better or more commonly present in the individual.

So, to sum up: when I refer to introversion as a trait, I refer to it as one's **dominant** temperamental state. Not a lack of extroversion, not the only way one can be, but simply the default setting for the individual in question.

Cool? Cool. Let's move ahead into learning more about what introversion really is and what it looks like in our field.

CHAPTER ONE
The Myth of Solitude

Welcome to the Struggle

So much of me wants to be lost in my grand ideas and reflections, away from the noise and urgency of other people, but I cannot escape the fact that growth invariably involves the messiness of genuine human contact and the struggles of intimacy." -Adam McHugh, *Introverts and the Church*

This dichotomy is all too real for introverts. We appreciate, and understand the need for, other people in order for us to thrive as individuals. But sometimes, it's just easier and more comfortable to be alone with our thoughts. Much of our lives~ with family, among friends, and especially at work ~ are occupied with the struggle between these two worlds.

I start with this quote and sentiment to illustrate the fact that it truly is a struggle. Many extroverts are of the belief that a preference for introversion is a preference for solitude. While this is true sometimes, it is rarely true all of the time. Dana, an extrovert who graciously agreed to contribute to this project, voiced a sentiment that I hear often when discussing ways to approach extroverts: *Right now if I know someone is an introvert, I almost approach him/her distantly because I don't want to scare 'em off.*

I appreciate Dana for being forthright in expressing this opinion, for she is not the only one that feels this way. In fact, I found a similar mentality expressed in the (in many ways shocking) volume *200 Best Jobs for Introverts*. This book, a volume in the Jist's Best Jobs series, includes categories for introverted jobseekers that include "20 Jobs with the Most Solitary Work", "20 Jobs With the Least Contact with Others", and "20 Jobs Most Removed From the Public."

I want to take a moment to let that information sink in.

First, let me dispel what this book is suggesting. Jist's authors seem to believe that "introvert-friendly work" and "solitary work" are one and the same. However, the ideal work for introverts typically is not work that completely isolates them from people. In fact, Laurie Helgoe believes that many of the fundamental elements of introversion make them ideally suited for service professions that allow them to work with people:

> We may pursue work for practical reasons or because we're good at something, or because we have a compelling vision of what the work will mean [...] we go into people work

because we can see within people.

Further, Marti Laney notes that the true nature of introverts allows them to be well suited for people-focused work:

> While it is true that introverts are focused on their own thoughts and feelings, they're also extremely interested in learning about *other people's* thoughts and feelings. (emphasis added)

Now, compare this pair of quotes to this one, noted student affairs practitioner Susan Komives' foreword to *Helping College Students: Developing Essential Support Skills For Student Affairs Practice*:

> In its most transcendent expression, the invitation "can you help me?" is an invitation into the head and the heart when a person is most open to examination, expresses a need to change, and is willing to risk moving from old ways of being to a new level of perspective or ability.

With a set of talents that allow introverts to see

deeply into the motivations and interests of others, and a legitimate desire to do so, why should they deny these feelings in favor of jobs that will purposefully prevent these sorts of exchanges? Yes, the Jist's book does come with a warning to the jobseeker that "the job should suit your whole personality- not just your introversion." I would say that a job should suit your whole personality, *including* your introversion. And as Susan Komives has eloquently just shown us, a job in student affairs can be that job!

The Purpose of Introvert Solitude

I want to talk about carbs for a moment. Stay with me, I promise there's a point.

Let's say I was to cook rice for lunch or dinner. I can start with a cup of rice and two cups of water. They can go in together, and cook for the recommended amount of time. I only buy brown rice, so let's say 35-45 minutes. No draining needed, because the rice absorbs the water. All it needs is a brief fluff when it's all done, and it's ready to serve.

Extroverts are like rice. They absorb what is around them without losing quality. They need a little less space to get going, and are fairly hardy for long periods of time.

Now think about the cooking process for pasta. One pound of pasta requires FIVE QUARTS of water! It cooks for less time (no more than ten minutes), and needs to be removed from the hot water before it's served.

Introverts are the pasta of the world. We need a lot more moving around room to effectively serve our purpose. We can't take the high heat as long as rice can. And, most important to this chapter, after a given amount of time we have to get out of the highly stimulated environment that is hot water. If we don't...well, I think we've all had overcooked pasta. It's simply not at its best when it gets too hot. And, as introverts, neither are we.

When you think about the office that you work in, perhaps the department, do you think introverts are allowed to be more like pasta? Or are they being prepared like rice? As you formulate an answer, consider the following criteria:
Do you have an open-office plan or cubicles, or are staff members in offices? If the latter is true, how is "closed-door" time perceived? Are students, staff members, or others coming to visit encouraged to set appointments, or are drop-in visits more encouraged? Are meetings planned, or are impromptu sessions called at will?

No answer to these questions is right or wrong, to be clear. However, there are some practices that are easier for extroverts to navigate than introverts. As such, their ability to work effectively can vary based on these factors.

When I first started out in my career as a professional, I longed for the day when I would be able to graduate from a receptionist's desk, and later a cubicle, to an office with a door. Yes, equating a door with prestige originally fueled some of the desire I felt for a door. But secretly, I longed

to have a door so I could close it. To most introverts, a closed door means time to relax, decompress, and to keep the "hot water" from getting in. Cubicles and open office plans are designed with the good intentions of keeping employees connected to each other, encouraging a collaborative and collegial spirit. While these elements can be fostered in an open environment, it wears on introverts a great deal.

Even once we ascend to a level where we're deemed worthy of a door, some departments and divisions believe that it should be left open. Closed doors aren't equated with peace, but with disengagement. An open door means we're friendly, ready to receive students and colleagues. A closed door looks, to some, standoffish and rude. Thus, even after we get the door that we so deeply need to preserve our energy and sanity, we're strongly discouraged from using it.

And even when we expect to be around people ~ for example, in meetings ~ sometimes these meeting opportunities pop up when we're neither prepared nor energized. The spontaneous meeting is the scourge of the introvert mind.

In an office potentially fraught with all of these concerns, its no wonder we sometimes feel beset by extroverted demands at times.

When I asked friends and colleagues what the most significant hallmark of their introversion was, one answer rose well above the others in its frequency: **a need to recharge**. To counter the occasionally overwhelming pace of daily life, introverts benefit most from time alone or in a quiet place to "power up" once again. Joanna speaks about her need to recharge, and says:

> As someone who identifies with the introversion preference I would say the trait that plays the biggest role in my life is how I re-energize or where I get my energy from, [...] I always need "me time" at some point during the day even if its just for a short amount of time. I like to have my quiet time and space to reflect in order to recharge.

Jessi echoes Joanna's sentiments and emphasizes the role of solitude in an effective recharge as she writes:

> I'm easily drained, and need to be virtually alone and doing almost nothing to accomplish a good recharge. This is obviously dependent upon what I've been doing and how familiar I am with the activity (work & commuting used to be draining, but I have it mostly under control now).

Jessi makes an excellent point about activities getting easier as they become more familiar. For me, public speaking has gradually become more comfortable, as I find the energizing pieces of the experience. But even after years of practice and exposure, it still gets tiring to do! We'll talk more about public speaking and introverts later on.

Even extroverts recognize the need for the introverts in their lives to take time for themselves to return refreshed and energized. Jason says this about his partner:

> I'm an extrovert in love with an introvert so I think about this a lot.
> I think [my partner]'s introversion manifests more in his need for quiet time. He's an intense dude and needs to get away from time to time. It's not that he's not social or doesn't like crowds; it's just that he needs to recharge and process in a safe, quiet space.

Getting a Good Charge

So in a world that tends to see alone time as synonymous with antisocial, even aloof behavior, how does one make time to get a full charge? Much like anything that requires a charge- a mobile device, your computer, anything with a battery- certain requirements must be fulfilled.

First and foremost, an introvert's recharge takes *time*. Think about your cell phone for just a moment. Much as we'd like to think that we could will our phones to hold a charge long enough to finish a task or a conversation, when the power is gone, it's gone. No amount of wishing or prayer can reverse it. Introverts are the same way. So even if a more extroverted person did want an introverted counterpart to come out after a long or particularly stimulating day, the introvert might literally not have it in him or her. The charge could take a few hours, like your laptop, or even a day or two; we're all different, and the time to recharge varies widely depending on the nature of the draining activity and the quality of the recharge.

That brings me to the next crucial element of a good recharge- *an outlet*. We all have our place where we can go that leaves us most relaxed. A park, the beach, or even a comfortable chair or bed. The place in question doesn't even need to be a physical place- the more bookish introverts could call the place that a good book takes them, their outlet. Our devices in need of recharge aren't nearly as picky, but the right environment can make a full recharge, or break it.

What would cause a "broken" opportunity to recharge? Consider what happens when we have a power cord that periodically shorts, or when we try to charge a phone when power is inconsistent. Not so effective, right? A *functioning outlet* is essential to a full charge; it's true of electronics, and it's true of people. What sorts of things cause the charge of an introvert to "short"? The answer the same for people as it is for electronics- anything that creates an interruption. Too little time between stimulating activities, people dropping in, or other disruptions to that time away from the grind will prevent a full recharge from happening. Monica F. affirms this sentiment, as she talks about what interruptions do to her ability to recharge:

> [...] I traits also make it hard for me to handle interruptions. As we all know, interruptions are a daily part of life, especially with motherhood and student affairs! Interruptions make me lose focus, energy, and momentum.

Why are interruptions so influential in disrupting the routine of introverts? The answer can be found, like so many other answers when referring to introverts, in the brain. Acetylcholine, an abundant hormone in the introverted brain, is responsible for our ability to concentrate deeply. Introverts have more acetylcholine in their brains than extroverts, whose actions are governed primarily by dopamine. It should also be noted that acetylcholine's path to the brain is longer than dopamine's path. A longer path means the flow of hormones is harder to "shut it down" when the brain has to quickly switch gears, as it does when you're interrupted. We'll talk more about acetylcholine when we discuss the myth of silence, but I did want to provide a primer here.

Up until this point, I've addressed the benefits of solitude for introverts. But I've said little to refute the aforementioned "myth of solitude." I want to do that now.

The Stealth Introvert

We traveled a lot as children. My father is a professor, and my sister and I were lucky to be able to occasionally travel with my parents when he delivered keynote lectures in other states and, eventually, other countries. When I was far younger, I used to disappear as we were boarding. Frantic, my parents would start searching for me, calling my name or (von Trapps and children of West African parentage will appreciate this) whistling. More often than not, I would turn up in a seat that appeared to be unoccupied, my tiny but unmistakable voice rising above the hustle and bustle of boarding rituals: "Hi, I'm Amma! Where are you going?"

Although I didn't seem to have an understanding that everyone on a place was going the *same* place, I can reflect on this experience and see that I had an understanding of what the true relationship between introverts and others can look like. This gregarious two-year-old version of me was ready to settle in and have a conversation. With a seemingly nonexistent understanding of the "stranger danger" concept, I singled out an individual. Just one. If this stranger looked nice, I was interested in getting to know him or her. But that being said, that conversation didn't usually last very long. I would get tired, be swooped up by my mom or dad, and returned to my rightful seat where I swiftly fell asleep. And *that* is the introverted part.

Introverts can talk to people. In fact, they are particularly skilled in having deep conversations with others because they are prone to reflection on the words and ideas of others, and to listen attentively as stories are being told. But that expends a tremendous amount of energy, and the exhaustion that quickly consumed my two-year-old body represents that well. I can tell you that there is a reason that I didn't start at the front of the plane and walk back gradually, trying to say hello to everyone. That simply wasn't in my nature, and still isn't. And yet I have friends who would truly enjoy such an activity!

Sophia Dembling writes in *The Introvert's Way* that "the not-so-shy introvert could be considered to have superior social skills to extroverts because they can accept attention without requiring it [...] I accept attention, I sometimes invite it, but I don't compete for it." And indeed, the socially accessible introvert (who I dub "the stealth introvert") has some advantages in many common situations in our field. These are the people who can maintain higher levels of small talk or strenuous social contact before shutting down completely. Yet, at some point, even they have to retire to recharge, and still favor more intentional and deep exchanges.

Cassidy, an introvert working in student activities, has found a way to create a look of stealth introversion in an environment that many quieter folk struggle with: conferences.

> I've found that one of our field's biggest introvert challenges - the conference - can be navigated by tapping into the one-on-one relationships that we introverts are really good at building. Leading up to a conference, I make an effort to reach out to colleagues who I haven't seen for some time or who I'd like to meet, and I try to break up the "crowded" parts of conferences with quiet lunch or coffee catch-up sessions one-on-one with friends and mentors.

Cassidy's version of being social is absolutely valid, and may not even be different from how our extroverted counterparts choose to navigate these same situations. Where we differ is in the *necessity* for these types of exchanges. In an environment where most days are characterized by a sea of people for long periods, even days on end, these purposeful and significant "get-away" moments are the lifeblood of the overwhelmed introvert.

I want to make a special note of a point that Cassidy made: connecting with people you'd *like* to meet. The explosion of student affairs presence on the Internet has made accessing colleagues from across the country far easier than it would have been ten to fifteen years ago. You may have found a few like-minded colleagues, or even kindred spirits, in your time online. Take the opportunity to transform these online relationships into "face to face" ones at conferences. (I say "face to face" because "in real life" feels wrong. The Internet is not the Matrix. It's real!) It has the benefit of being an exchange you can ease into, because you have some familiarity with the person and his or her personality. Don't pass up the chance to put a life-sized face to a name, screen name, or Twitter handle.

But these sojourns, with whomever and however quick, cannot sustain the conference experience. Part of the value of these experiences is the ability to make brand new connections, and you will find few greater opportunities than a conference to meet so many people from so many walks of life and with such diverse knowledge. So how does the introvert navigate such a situation? "Don't give into the butterflies, find them!" Break through that natural instinct to bask in solitude- fortune favors the bold, and your time and energy will be rewarded. And once you break through, you'll be further favored when you use your unique and insightful voice. How, you may ask? Read on, and more will be revealed.

INsights

⇒ Introverts *need* solitude, in a very real way neurologically and physiologically.

⇒ Needing time for solitude is completely normal. They are needed to protect your ability to process information, to be present in any given moment, and to be productive and at your best when interacting with others.

⇒ Remind those around you, however you see fit, that needing solitude doesn't mean *not* needing relationships!

⇒ The line between "acting extroverted" and "acting introverted" is less real than we think. Introversion doesn't leave any skill or behavior out of reach! Some tasks will simply take more energy for you to complete; accept this, and do what you can to build your energy stores accordingly.

⇒ When working with students, make sure that

programs like training, retreats, and other long-term or large-scale events include time for solitude. The impact of the information being shared will be more evident when time is provided for those renewing moments to happen organically.

CHAPTER TWO
The Myth of Silence

"You're an introvert? I never would have guessed; you speak so well!"

Titles of other books on introversion have "Quiet" in them for a reason. It is part of the introverted nature to be quieter than our extroverted counterparts. However, our quiet nature should not be mistaken for so many of the qualities that are ascribed to it. We are not judgmental, aloof, antisocial, dangerous, or free from thoughts. In fact, that last part is likely why introverts seem so comfortable in perceived silence- because to us, it's not quiet! One of Marti Laney's younger clients had a mother who was deeply concerned about how reserved she seemed. When confronted about her seemingly standoffish behavior, she responded, "I didn't realize! It's *never* quiet in my head!" Put another way, pastor Adam McHugh said about the introverted mind, "Introverts often give off the appearance of calmness, while self-doubt and anxiety rumbles around inside of us." The interior chaos is well hidden behind a facade of serenity.

Herein lies a chasm between an introvert's understanding of his or her 'wiring', and how he or she is perceived. To illustrate the difference, I'd like to utilize the analogy of a clock. Extroverts process information fairly openly, with their thought paths often revealed verbally. When trying to make a decision, they may talk out the many options. A financial aid advisor preparing for an information fair may walk around his or her office, listing everything that needs to come along. Think of an extrovert as an analog clock. A clock can tell you time, but you can also tell, because of the second hand, how it arrives at the time it displays. The gears and cogs powering its movement may be visible and audible as the time ticks away, betraying the inner workings at play.

Conversely, introverts operate like a digital clock. You see the time that it displays, but very little of how it arrived at that display. Even when the computer chips or transistors powering this clock are visible, the many binary decisions being made inside are imperceptible to the casual observer. Decision-making is internalized, finding its way out of the brain in writing. Preparation to leave the office with lots of items may leave an introverted advisor checking items off a list, or mentally talking to him or herself to ensure nothing gets left behind.

This difference in conversational style is profound, even from childhood. Marti Laney provides this description of the ideal conversational pace for introverted children, a style that many will carry into adulthood:

> Their brains are made for lingering over thoughts and feelings and achieving a deeper understanding of a subject. They speak more slowly and lose their place if they are interrupted. They listen, ask questions, and consider the other person's ideas.

Compare the introverted desire to speak more slowly, speak without interruption, and dig deep into conversations of interest, to our fast-paced and information-rich society, and you may see why the introverted way of life collides so clumsily with the extroverted ideal.

So why do some individuals need to talk their way through life, while others seem exhausted by the prospect? The short answer: science. But wait, there's more.

The Most Science-y Part of the Book

There are two chemicals in the brain that control our response to stimuli: dopamine and acetylcholine. The former is responsible for the "fight or flight" response: it gets our hearts racing, blood pumping faster, and provides the rush of energy needed to flee the threat at hand. If it were powering a car, it'd be most like the turbo boost available on some sports cars.

The latter is responsible for calming us down and enabling our ability to focus deeply and concentrate. It also is responsible for our partial paralysis and REM sleep each night. If dopamine powers the turbo boost, acetylcholine functions much like cruise control. All humans have some level of both dopamine and acetylcholine coursing through their brains. However, recent research has determined that the brains of those who differ in temperament also differ in the levels of these hormones and the dominant pathways on which these hormones travel. If you guessed that extroverts have more dopamine and that introverts have more acetylcholine...bingo. You nailed it. Here are a few reasons why these hormonal differences are important:

> **Introverts are chemically equipped to concentrate.** Acetylcholine, as I mentioned previously, is the hormone that allows deep concentration. This explains the introverted tendency to learn a great deal about areas of interest with relative ease. But from an office standpoint, it works against us for a key element to student affairs: interruption. Variety in a workday keeps things interesting, as do unanticipated challenges that arise each day, courtesy of our students. But after these impromptu meetings, student crises, or last-minute errands, introverts have a harder time returning to their regularly scheduled programming.
>
> The neural pathway on which acetylcholine travels is longer than the one on which dopamine travels. This makes it harder to get started again once it is preempted by a situation that creates a flow of dopamine. A chemical aversion to interruption can be even more difficult for introverts who work

in cubicles or as a part of open-office plans. A lack of a barrier to interruptions can keep them operating at a suboptimal rate.

Acetylcholine releases more delicate stimulation than dopamine. The stimulation that acetylcholine does provide is a more subdued form of energy than that which dopamine stimulates. It can easily be fueled by quiet conversation, by the noises of nature, or an easygoing conversation with a close friend. This form of stimulation is simply not enough to satisfy the dopamine-fueled brains of most extroverts, who need the greater rush of more animated exchanges and the constant drone of a TV or radio in the background. Interestingly enough, this pattern switches when it's time to drift off to sleep; introverts may like music or a white noise machine to drown out the whirring of their own thoughts, but too much noise or stimulation keeps some extroverts from sleeping.

What does this mean for a work environment? It means that some common situations that we find ourselves in in student affairs- divisional meetings, conference socials, panel or roundtable discussions- work against the natural wiring of introverts participating in these events. As such, they are more likely to find themselves at a loss to speak because their brain is working to mitigate the overstimulation they are feeling. *Overstimulation*—not disinterest or flightiness— are the likely cause of those words that leave our mind the moment we're called on, or have trouble remembering the names of people we're engaged in conversation with.

The introverted brain is more active in sections responsible for planning and deliberation. The introvert's talent for concentration and preference for stability makes them ideal planners and deliberators. A natural thirst for information drives them to make decisions based on as many of the facts, opinions, and contributing factors as possible. Additionally, the long pathway of acetylcholine means that they need more time to make decisions, making sure that their brain is not rushed to catch up. This differs somewhat from the decision-making abilities of the extrovert. I don't wish to say that extroverts don't deliberate over big decisions; that would be a gross generalization. But what I will say is that the quick pathway of dopamine, combined with heightened comfort with uncertainty and their ease in talking out decisions, better equips extroverts to make quick decisions.

For students who enter our offices in a blur of frustration or emotion, needing a quick answer, it can be hard for introverts to respond with an equal sense of urgency. They may be tempted to ask for more information, request that the student slow down when explaining the situation, or even ask for more time to render a decision. Understandably, this is not an ideal way of working. Supervisors of introverts would be wise to provide their supervisees as much time as possible to make decisions, lest a feeling of duress affect their decision making process. But we'll talk more about how supervision can affect introverts later on.

I could talk all day about how acetylcholine governs the introverted mind, but I will instead refer you to

Laney's books *The Introvert Advantage, The Hidden Gifts of the Introverted Child,* and *The Introvert and Extrovert in Love*; more information on all these books can be found in the "On the Shoulders of Giants" section at the conclusion of this book.

More Information Required

I think before I speak. To many, the more accurate way to phrase that would be, "Amma, you *overthink* before you speak." Perhaps that's true. But a hallmark of my communications with friends, family, coworkers and others I interact with is thoughtfulness. Eric, a social media strategist, has referred to such deliberate thinking as the "toy boat" strategy: before typing something, he advises you to say the phrase "toy boat" three times fast. Aside from having just attempted to say a nearly impossible phrase, you will have slowed your mind down enough to really think about what you're going to type. But I find that my whole life as a communicator is a series of "toy boat" moments. I naturally build this thinking time into my exchanges, regardless of the medium. As I've learned through my research and discussions from fellow introverts, this is not a trait specific to me.

Joe, a first-year specialist at a community college said it best when he noted:

> I know when I e-mail an extrovert, I'm going to get an e-mail back that may be short, may be long, but it is full of thoughts as if it their fingers couldn't keep up with the thought. Punctuation, spelling, grammar, none of that matters because I'm sure they assume I know what they are trying to say [...] Now when I have an introvert in my network, I know and half expect the response to come a day or two later. When that indicator pops up that I have a new message or my phone shows new mail, I'm excited. Why? Because I know one of the strengths of introversion is deep reflection and thought into what they say and how they say it. I don't expect novels back, shoot I've gotten some one-liners that have left me wanting to write pages in response. The quality of introversion is the ability, and sometimes need, to shut off and put themselves so deep into thought about a topic that the insight and thought-provoking response that comes out is well worth the wait.

Joe went on to say that he recognized that this could be a generalization of the two types; I respect and agree with that assessment. Sometimes, you know just what to say and how to say it, and the waiting period isn't as necessary or as long. But you can bet that whatever response is sent, it will have been deliberated upon and carefully crafted. This is why introverts can sometimes have trouble responding to spontaneous questions. The requests of "let me get back to you" or "can I think about that a bit more?" aren't designed to stall a response, but to allow a response time to fully materialize. Even when working with students, or at times when a response is a matter of citing policy, additional thought may be needed. Be patient with this need. It will be rewarded.

A common misconception about introverts and surprises surrounds their shyness, or a need to have as much information as possible. While these ideas have the potential to be true, an equally likely reason for their dislike of surprises is the lack of preparation time associated with such events. Even in day-to-day conversations, many introverts would prefer to sit in silence and ponder a question, while others with more extroverted tendencies will speak as they assemble a response. Lisa, a student services professional from Toronto said it quite eloquently when she termed introverts "powerful masters of the silent space, not rushing to fill emptiness with noise."

An area of significant interest for me is employee selection and onboarding, and creating understanding environments for introverted candidates is very important to me. One element of this project is helping colleagues reframe our long-standing ideas about the interview process. Some who interview with us may not be the most dynamic or charismatic speakers. And for a society that evolved to appreciate charisma as a means of uniting people, that's a hard break to make. The need for introverts to process quietly at a time when answers are expected (such as an interview) can have its drawbacks. Too often, we have been indoctrinated to believe that silence as an initial response to a question means that the person being questioned doesn't know the answer. I would like to pose an inverse theory; the introvert knows the answer, but is trying to determine the best way to express it. So I try to direct my colleagues and students toward other measures of success besides the ability to answer an interview question quickly and perfectly. *Let your candidate take a beat.* The insight you receive at the end of that pause could be wonderful, but those good things will only come to those who wait.

Speak Up! Or, Introverts and Public Speaking

> "I could stand up in front of hundreds of people and preach a sermon without nervousness, but I often stumbled through the greeting time afterward because my energy resolves were dry."

> "You're an introvert? But you can speak so well in front of people!"

Does that first quote sound like you? Does that second quote sound like many of your friends or your family? It might surprise you to know just how true both of these statements can be, even as they seem to crash against each other in a clunky or discordant way. The former is true, in that the world of public speaking is actually quite well suited to the talents and abilities of introverts. And the latter is true, as a quite common misconception that extroverts have about their quiet counterparts. I want to use this pair of quotes to frame my discussion on introverts and public speaking- and no, the two are not diametric opposites!

Adam McHugh is a former campus minister, current pastor, and author of the tremendously informative *Introverts in the Church*, the book from which the first quote was taken. In it, he unpacks the many assumptions made about evangelism and what it takes to be a "good member" of the church. He speaks about an institution that values highly the ability to effortlessly interact broadly with those in the community, speak quickly and without hesitation, and be forthright in approaching those who we want to understand us. Sound familiar? So many times as I absorbed McHugh's words, I felt that "student affairs" and "evangelical ministry" could easily have been interchangeable terms.

One place that Adam wrote about feeling at home was on the pulpit. To our more extroverted counterparts, this seems crazy. Speaking up? In front of all those people? That doesn't make sense! To be fair, sometimes this assumption is correct.

For shy introverts, this public speaking ability doesn't always come as easily. Here again, there is a distinction between shy and introverted. I've heard this distinction voiced several ways, but I appreciate the way that Susan Cain voiced it best in *Quiet*: "Shyness is inherently painful; introversion is not."

For shy introverts, the fear of judgment that is accompanied with putting your words and opinions on a larger stage can force them to shrink in the presence of a spotlight. Frankly, that is a fear shared by all *shy* people, NOT all introverted people. For those who are introverted, but not shy, this fear doesn't prevent us from taking center stage *in the service of something greater*. Why the qualifier? Introverts don't tend to seek attention for its own sake. Their inward orientation avoids attention-grabbing maneuvers. If their public speaking can help someone, introduce a topic they are passionate about, or spark a meaningful discussion, however, they're generally willing to let that spotlight shine.

As an example, an introverted academic advisor may have no trouble speaking to parents and students en masse during information sessions, because it is in the service to something greater- to present information and create an understanding of the admissions process. As student affairs practitioners, we tend to evangelize a little differently, and our pulpits vary wildly depending on what our jobs entail and what element of the student experience we'll be speaking to. There are a few more reasons that introverts have a distinct advantage in public speaking- if you're an introvert, keep these in mind if you're struggling to decide how you feel about speaking up; if you're an extrovert, use these tips to help you remember that your introverted friends and colleagues are not shaking leaves! We can speak up when the situation calls for it!

> **Preparation:** The type of public speaking that is typical in student affairs favors preparation. The ability to amass and organize information, and then package it for public consumption, is a skill that many introverts already possess. As such, they will be more willing to flex their public speaking muscles when the opportunity favors prior preparation. If our aforementioned admissions counselor had a good idea of what needed to be covered, had adequate

time to prepare her lecture, and had notes handy in case of emergency, temperament would be no obstacle to her success!

Lack of Interruption: Given the way in which the introverted brain is wired, interruptions are uncomfortable and can even hamper an individual's ability to communicate effectively. But most public speeches- information sessions, conference presentations, the increasing utility of TED talks in education -- interruptions are unlikely, or can be minimized by requesting that questions be moved to the end. Conversation, as we all know, doesn't always work like this. The threat of an interruption while speaking in a conversation looms large for introverts, so they may be reluctant to contribute when speaking amongst others, at times avoiding it all together. But in a venue that minimizes interruptions, and along with them the fear of losing a train of thought or momentum of discussion, the quieter members of our staff can truly shine. Admissions information sessions, structured with questions addressed at the conclusion of prepared remarks, are an ideal way for our admissions counselor to be able to be in the public eye on behalf of, and in service to, her office.

Knowledge and Excitement: If you ever want to see an introvert truly come alive, ask him or her about something they're interested in or knowledgeable about. A person who may have previously appeared to be standoffish, inattentive, or disengaged, will practically light up. And those of us who are known for never talking may now never stop! Introverts are happy to share the information that otherwise will bounce around inside their heads, if they feel as though someone wants to know. They are comfortable speaking about these areas of interest or expertise because they can speak authoritatively, and that provides a level of comfort that doesn't always show itself in situations where they are less sure. That is not to say that introverts fear being wrong; we all, introverts and extroverts alike, understand that it will happen from time to time and can accept that fact. However, the impact of being seen as wrong stays with many introverts much longer. To put it another way: introverts aren't afraid of being wrong, they're afraid of *what being wrong will make them look like.* This fear is mitigated when they feel confident that they can address what curveballs may come their way. Armed with the understanding that we are good at our jobs, and know the answers to any questions that may arise, will make public speaking all the easier for our admissions counselor, or anyone else serving in a similar capacity.

Given that successful introverted public speaking favors preparation, little interruption, and a combination of enthusiasm and comfort with material being presented, it may still surprise you to know that some of America's most beloved actors are introverted. Yes, despite the constant need for self-promotion and the ubiquitous public eye, actors like Will Ferrell and Julia Roberts have thrived in a very public profession. The latter is well known in the industry for the naps she takes during breaks on set, saying that she couldn't get through the day without them. I only wish that student affairs was a field so amenable to this practice, for I know many who would take full advantage of, and be far better for, it!

McHugh writes later in *Introverts in the Church* about the difference between public speaking as a form of communication, and the conversational interactions that are more likely to trip up the introverted:

> I feel that I am skilled in the "big" communication events -- preaching and teaching, casting vision, leading meetings -- but I struggle with "small" communication- small talk, saying the little things that make people feel known and appreciated, expressing interest in the details of people's lives, or even returning phone calls promptly.

There is a lot of truth to this for many introverts. Small communication tests the malleability of the introverted spirit. Our internal, idea-focused nature makes the concepts we speak on in "big" venues easier for us to articulate. Big stages are easier to communicate on, for the reasons listed above and countless others, than the smaller ones that

McHugh labors over. But it is important to note, those committed to not letting their introversion define them do labor through these struggles. He goes on to say,

> Aware of our proclivity for enigmatic silence, introverted leaders act in love and understanding toward extroverts when we practice communication that is unnatural to us. We give more feedback and affirmation than we think is necessary; we repeat ourselves, even several times when making an important point; we contort our faces and gesticulate; and we sometimes give expression to incomplete thoughts to let extroverts know that we're engaged in the conversation.

This passage is one of my favorites from McHugh, because it articulates habits that I know I've picked up in order to better fit in conversations in "mixed company". I am the most comfortable expressing a thought when it's fully baked, as they say, but I know this isn't always the way that those around me operate. Though it pains me to do so at times, I have trained myself to take an idea that isn't quite done to a more extroverted coworker or my extroverted director, to fit their distinctly different styles. But I have found value in that practice as well. While it isn't always the most comfortable thing for me to do, I've found it to be productive!

Introverts who allow the struggle to "leave their heads" to overcome them miss the opportunity to garner input and seek perspective from those around them. And some of the best initiatives in our office have come from a nearly baked idea that one individual brought to the table and allowed the rest of us to tweak. There is value in stepping out of our rich inner world sometimes, so taking that step is uncomfortable but necessary.

Introversion and Shyness

> I don't want to make the mistake of equating introversion with shyness [...] and assuming that an introvert will not make his or her voice heard; rather, is the introvert is forced to process in an extroverted manner, they may not have the opportunity to do their best work and may not have arrived at something they feel is of value to share. - Curtis T.

Of the myths associated with introversion, this is one of the most omnipresent. If you're introverted, you must be shy, right? I mean, you don't talk, you don't avoid social situations, which means shy!

Well...no.

In my research for this book, I was presented with a great deal of insight into the difference between shyness and introversion. But Marti Laney puts it most elegantly when she says, "introversion is who you are, while shyness is what you think others think you are." That is to say, introversion is a construct that is internally oriented; shyness is one that is externally constructed. Introversion is a conscious decision to retreat inward, knowing that is the most energized stance for productivity. Comparatively, shyness is a state of being where that drive inward is driven less by you as a decision, and more by others and the fear associated with their judgment or opinion. To borrow a metaphor from *Introverts and the Church*, "we don't avoid social situations like we would a trip to the dentist" (as some do out of fear, as is the case with social endeavors and shyness), "but sometimes we avoid them like we would exercise, because we lack the energy for them" (as some do out of a lack of energy, as is the case with social encounters and introversion).

Further, shyness is a construct that affects people on all points of the temperament spectrum. One of the most insightful contributors to this book, Jessi, describes herself as "incredibly shy". She is extraordinarily thoughtful and well spoken when given the opportunity to express herself in writing, as she does on her blog and has when answering questions for me in my research stages. But "shy" is also a word that Curtis, whose quote opens this section, uses to describe himself. Another term he uses to describe himself? Extrovert. Yes, shy extroverts are a thing! It is entirely possible to be energized by people, and also feel tentative or fearful when approaching your potential sources of energy.

Another essential distinction between introversion and shyness: the former is an immutable element of personality, while the latter can be overcome through repeated exposure to scary situations or unfamiliar people. Shyness is a sensation driven largely by fear or discomfort. Like many fears or uncomfortable sensations, familiarity breeds an easing of those symptoms. And although this is true for introverts as well (that is, familiarity in overwhelming situations can mitigate some ill effects), once the critical mass of energy expenditure is reached, that discomfort will not get better.

Curtis makes an outstanding point about the assumption that introverts will not make their voices heard when needed. Yes, speaking up to address a concern is difficult for both those who are shy and those who are introverts, more so than it is for those who are not shy or are extroverts. But the medium an introvert is given to express concerns or frustrations, whether the introvert is shy or not, makes a difference. How many times do we hear after a meeting, "come talk to me if you have concerns"? Further, how often are we prompted to give feedback or address problems in a meeting in real time? There is nothing inherently wrong with either of these strategies, for they allow issues to be addressed quickly. However, they are disadvantageous strategies for the introvert.

Introverts require time to gather their thoughts on

an issue, and additional time to determine how to express those concerns. Those who are internally focused place a tremendous premium on how ideas are presented when they do finally cross the threshold into the outside world. As such, the introvert's problem with speaking up in a meeting isn't fear of speaking, but fear of speaking incompletely or incorrectly. Thus, those in the position to run meetings or otherwise solicit feedback should keep this in mind and offer additional means for attendees or participants to chime in. Consider sending agendas out early and soliciting questions or concerns in writing prior to the meeting, or prompting attendees a few days afterward to follow up with emails. When a culture of written and delayed feedback is encouraged, you'll likely hear more from introverts, allowing their valuable and carefully considered input to be included in the discussion.

With a preference for asynchronous communication and venues that allow for written thought, it should surprise few that introverts come alive on social media. And why shouldn't they? Most social media platforms allow you to respond to conversations or threads on your own time, and are forgiving of the time an individual may need to ponder and craft a fitting response. It presents enough information about the individuals you're speaking with that you can approach those you share common interests with, with a reasonable level of confidence that you will get along. And if the socializing gets overwhelming, walking away from the screen is far less anxiety-inducing than leaving a crowded party or getting up to leave a meeting. Keep this information in mind as you interact with students in asynchronous media. There are some who you may have a hard time interacting with face-to-face, but are far easier to understand and reach from behind a screen. While there's not a great deal of actual data on this introverted preference for social media (most of my observations are anecdotal), I'm very interested to see how those of different temperaments utilize social media differently.

The Vacuum of Quiet

> "One of the risks of being quiet is that other people can fill your silence with their own interpretations. You're bored. You're depressed. You're shy. You're judgmental.

> You have nothing to say. [...] Nature abhors a vacuum, and when other people can't read us, they write their own story- not always one that we would choose or that's true to who we are."
> -Sophia Dembling, *The Introvert's Way*

The introvert's way of relating to others generally requires that they stand in the background, observing and listening. But for people who don't traditionally behave that way, those preferences will be perceived differently than we might intend. Chances are, if you asked the overwhelming majority of introverts why they silence themselves, the answers wouldn't include the assumptions listed above.

Susan Cain's Introvert Manifesto is comprised of what she calls "Sixteen Things I Believe". Twelfth on that list is the statement, "Quiet leadership is not an oxymoron." And indeed, saying little is not the same as saying nothing. Introverts have a wealth of wisdom, creativity, competence, and knowledge to share with the world. When given enough time, a comfortable venue, and the confidence and understanding of those around them, they will share it. Once they do, you may actually struggle to stop the flow of contribution! But it starts with understanding. Another myth that introverts need understanding to overcome is their perceived need to separate themselves from a group. Ahead, we'll address that myth, its origins, and what the reality actually looks like.

INsights

⇒ Introverts tend to speak at the end of a thought, while extroverts (by their very nature) speak at the beginning. Remind those around you of this fact by saying things like "Could I have a moment to consider that?" or "Let me think that over."

⇒ The introvert need to be prepared is a very real one; do what you can to articulate that need for those you work with, students and staff alike.

⇒ You will have moments of natural excitement over topics you are highly interested in or very knowledgeable about. Don't hold back in these moments, for this is where you truly shine. Share your knowledge with whoever needs to hear it!

⇒ When working with students, make sure to create space in meetings, events, classes, and the like. Even introverted professionals have a way of equating eloquence and gregariousness with high performance. Remember that some students need more time to provide evidence of their brilliance-you're better equipped to give it to them than anyone else.

CHAPTER THREE
The Myth of Separation

Introverts are not immune to loneliness. We can be lonely surrounded by people if we haven't found anyone to connect with. We also can get lonely if we allow the momentum of solitude to override our natural need for companionship. -Sophia Dembling, The Introvert's Way

Aloof. Standoffish. Selfish. All of these are words that have, at one point or another, been associated with introversion. The introvert's gradual method of warming to someone before bringing them into their inner circle can seem to move at a glacial pace for an extrovert who is eager to jump in and make new friends. But, as extrovert Jeff (you'll learn more about him shortly) notes, these adjectives are ill placed at best, and blatantly untrue at worst:

> What frustrates me the most about peoples' views of introversion is the notion that introverts don't like people and want to be alone. All the time. Heaven forbid if an introvert is in the vicinity of another human being, their head might explode. Introverts don't watch the movie *Cast Away* and think that's a new career goal. Introverts like people too! In fact, they may like people *more* than us extroverts do (gasp!). While we're off putting on a show and dazzling groups of

people en masse, introverts are having a one on one interaction, getting to know someone on a deeper level. They're developing a meaningful relationship, investing in that person's life, and getting energized by that connection they are making. And that moment is more real, valuable, and inspiring than introverts are given credit for.

Jeff is absolutely correct; introverts are not without a need to connect with those around them. But those connections are made sparingly and extremely purposefully. And despite what you may think, many of these connections are made "across temperamental lines." I've found that some of my strongest relationships at work have been built with extroverts- they help us find ways to voice our opinions and concerns, and we can help them appreciate quieter moments and teach them to slow down when needed. Think of the benefits of extroverts from the introduction- any introvert open to receiving those benefits can find a friend for life in a temperamental counterpart, be it in a meeting or office setting, or networking at parties or conferences.

The Importance of Allies

Statistically speaking, at least one of the people with whom you've previously connected is an extrovert. Have this person work the proverbial room with you. This partner can break the ice where you may struggle, connect the dots between you and the people you meet, and encourage you to step out of your comfort zone. If this is a person who knows you well, this buddy could also help you monitor your energy level, creating an exit point for a conversation if you feel tired or unable to continue. Having extroverted friends who understand you is an invaluable resource; don't be afraid to let them help you at times like this! As an example, I'd like to share a story about a fun extrovert in my life who you just heard from.

Jeff said the word "penis" in class. I told him not to several times before it happened, and honestly thought he said it on purpose. But the look of shock on his face after he said it proved that there was no way that word was in his plan. And yet, there it was. Out in the atmosphere, never to be taken back. Our class, and in particular our professor, looked equally shocked. He attempted to backtrack. His "solution"? "Y'know, where your 'P' comes out." Sigh.

It was the spring of 2010, our first year in graduate school, and he was part of a group presenting on the Myers Briggs Type Indicator to our Student Development Theory class. And to be fair, the actual word used was "P-ness". In attempting to explain the tendencies of Judgers and Perceivers, he chose this way to express the tendencies of the latter. But this slip of the tongue shouldn't surprise anyone in the slightest, and likely surprises few that know him. In addition to being a perceiver, known for their cavalier nature and willingness to work without a plan, Jeff is one of my poster children for extroversion and earned a post as a panelist in this book for that very reason.

In spite of our many differences, we bonded quickly as we joined the University of South Florida College Student Affairs class of 2011. As we continued to discover common interests including but far from limited to collegiate a cappella, Walt Disney World, reading, and sandals, we became essentially inseparable. However, we at first clashed wildly on how to get work done. Attempts to study together would occasionally be thwarted by requests for music (his) or a need to set and adhere to deadlines (mine). Different work styles and approaches to social situations didn't keep us from growing close as friends, and eventually as collaborators on projects. And with a few stipulations, including one stating that he was no longer permitted to present on Judgers and Perceivers, we put together a presentation that started to change the way I looked at temperament.

"The Storm is Coming: Managing Conflict in Your Organization" was developed a year after the aforementioned penis debacle, and was designed for student groups to help them understand that differences in style don't have to hamper a good working relationship. As you might gather from the name, it utilized the Myers Briggs Type Indicator in concert with Tuckman's model to demonstrate how understanding of temperament can aid good group work. Our take: if it works for us, two wildly different personalities, it can work for you too! And indeed, as we got more practiced in delivering the presentation, the banter and our ability to help students process their own types came more and more easily. Simply put, the more often we gave the presentation together, the easier it was to believe the message that we were professing.

I often hold Jeff up as an example of an extrovert that "gets" introversion. When going into battle, it's always best to have an ally. And while graduate school is far from a battle, the constant group work, presentations, and networking opportunities are far from the comfort zone of the quieter among us. But from Jeff, there was never a push to participate more than I was comfortable, to stay out later than I could handle, or to talk to more people than I'd like. In fact, he was often the one to offer me an out when he could tell I was reaching my threshold. Despite previous discussion about his definitive Perceiver status, he is one of the most thoughtful people I know...in behavior, that is!

Prominent literature on temperament has pitted introverts and extroverts against each other, insisting that their natures are simply too different to be understood. But there are kindred spirits, as I hope to have shown in discussing my friend Jeff.

> While extroverts commonly feel loneliness when others are *absent*, introverts can feel

> most lonely when others are *present*, because ours is the aching loneliness of not being known or understood. -Adam McHugh

As we ponder the significance of a need for separation in ourselves, it should also be noted that we have students who may have needs for similar time away from others. Historically, this sort of separation has been viewed as unnatural, symptomatic of something horribly wrong, and something to actively be combated. What separation may actually be is a need for a select few experiences, ones that provide the depth they need to thrive. My own "resident extrovert" (more on that later), Jeff, beautifully encapsulated how our preparation programs and job training encourage perpetuation of the extrovert ideal:

> For introverts, breadth is not important; depth is. Yet in our residence halls, if a student doesn't have his/her door open every waking moment, that student is a recluse. If he/she can't make it to the athletic event, comedian, RA program, AND their study group, then he/she is "not involved enough" at the university. We spend more time

telling students what they should be interested in instead of asking what they are getting meaning out of. Extraverts love bouncing from event to event, making their appearances, being seen, and adding things to their list of titles at the end of their email signatures (we've all seen it). Introverts find meaning in other ways, and focus on the depth of their interactions and their experiences. Then we tell them they're not doing "enough."

How often have we ascribed isolation, maladjustment, apathy, or laziness to students that we see sparingly? Further, and of equal importance, how often do we attribute those traits to colleagues who behave in the same way? Individuals of all temperaments are guilty for making these assumptions of those who aren't always present, but sometimes this alleged separation merits a second look.

When looking at just how different people can be, it is tempting to paint a portrait of them as definitively introverted or absolutely extroverted. But rather than looking at those qualities as two opposite poles, I prefer to think of them as two sides of the same coin. And so does Carl Jung, who famously said during a 1957 conversation with Dr. Richard Evans in reference to the temperament scale he designed, "There is no such thing as a pure extrovert or a pure introvert. Such a man would be in the lunatic asylum."

Too often I've participated in an activity at a conference, during a meeting, or even once at church, where the person leading has instructed us to "do something the introverts will be uncomfortable with: talk to someone", or some similar set of instructions. My fear is that the understanding there is an often-highlighted myth about introverts: *introverts don't like people*. I am here to tell you that is not always true.

Inter-Temperament Love

In my research for this book, I came across several examples of "inter-temperamental love." Take, for example, Kelley, an introvert who often copes with her hectic life at work by spending time with her extroverted husband:

A[nother] strategy I use for working in student affairs and in my personal life, is my extrovert husband. I am one of the many introverts who married an extrovert, and with much intentional communication, we can be very supportive of the other's needs [...] Here's the other great part about being married to an extrovert - when we are in large groups or spending extended amounts of time with others - he naturally carries the conversation and keeps the momentum of the group energized and positive! I never feel the pressure to entertain others or keep conversation going when we are together, which is a huge relief for an introvert. I can lean on him and allow him to take the lead in his natural and preferred environment. This works in both social and work settings when it is appropriate to invite partners to events. I am very thankful for my extrovert husband, and the introvert/extrovert union truly can work!

Dana, an extrovert married to an introvert, echoed the ability for such relationships to work:

> My husband struggles in social settings with a lot of unfamiliar people. He just doesn't have a good time. I think we've both rubbed off on each other because I don't like large group outings like I used to, and he likes doing things with bigger groups now. I think we counterbalanced each other. Still, if there's a party with a lot of unfamiliar, he gravitates towards the people he knows. He will be polite if someone new says hello but won't go out of his way to ask questions or start conversations. That's where I come in.

While the testimonies of Kelley and Dana aren't strictly professional, I suspect that they are indicative of a more significant trend. Whether you call it work/life balance, work/life negotiation, or some other term to express the interplay between our personal and professional realms, introverts may use this time away from their work to decompress, understand, and make sense of life differently than extroverts do. Introverts may need a more explicit separation between their "work" lives and their "home" lives than their extroverted counterparts do. Of course, this is not to say that introverts cannot be successful in professional roles where these elements are intertwined. It is, however, worthy of note that these roles may wear on them more significantly than they would an extrovert.

There is also another potential contributor to the myth of separation, through a lens that divorces it from the idea of separating from people. If you recall, the operative element of being introverted is not an issue of relationships with people, but with overstimulation. Introverts struggle when they are stimulated to a point of discomfort. But when in a room with people, people are not the only element contributing to the environment. Rooms have lighting. They have noise levels. They have temperatures. Any excess stimulation pertaining to these factors could just as easily cause an introvert to become overloaded. Laurie Helgoe notes in her research that while not all introverts are what can be called "highly sensitive," many highly sensitive individuals are also introverts. What does this mean? This means that the introvert who has become uncomfortable in an environment could be reacting to overstimulation from the people in the room...or could be doing so because the room is too loud, too cold or too warm, or too bright. I don't want to overcomplicate this issue, or introduce too many additional variables to our discussion; if you're interested in learning more about high sensitivity, or Sensory-Processing Sensitivity, the work of Laurie Helgoe and Elaine Aron can give you more information.

So it would appear that the myth of separation is rather a misunderstanding of what type of separation is truly needed. Introverts don't need separation from others in an isolating fashion. Rather, they work best when able to form a few deep relationships that inspire them to do their best work. They also work best when given the opportunity to escape that work setting at some point to reflect, recharge, and find meaning in their day-to-day functions.

In setting straight the myths that we've covered up to this point, I hope that my contributors and I have been able to show you what the ideal conditions are for introverts. By explaining the motivation, both socially and scientifically, behind our often-misunderstood nature, I hope that you can better understand yourself (if you're an introvert) or a seemingly enigmatic introvert in your life (if you're an extrovert). But as we've all learned in life, ideal conditions don't always exist. In fact, they rarely do. So now we'll talk about what happens when our conditions fight with our ability to be authentically introverted.

INsights

⇒ Introverts and extroverts work incredibly well together. The synergy that comes from the complementary elements of their personalities and natural strengths can lead to success, learning, and sometimes even love.

⇒ Again, no activities are inherently "introverted" or "extroverted." Rather, there are activities that are better suited to each type. Balanced events, leadership roles, or learning opportunities will feature a mix of activities that appeal to both styles.

⇒ When working with students, make sure to educate students on the features of each type and how they might appeal to students with differing styles. Helping them understand one another can provide a powerful opportunity for them to build strong and balanced teams on their own.

⇒ If given the opportunity to pair students who have been educated on temperament, consider creating "mixed pairs." They often appreciate the opportunity to have a team that can effectively address the many sorts of people they'll encounter.

CHAPTER FOUR
Behind the Mask

Now that we've discussed at length what introversion is, and - equally importantly - what it isn't, I'd like to turn my attention to one way in which many of us have been trained to deal with it: *masking*. What do I mean by masking? This refers to all the ways that we respond when we allow ourselves to give in to the demands of extroverts, our concessions to phrases like "you're leaving the party already? We just got here!" or "Oh no, you *can't* miss this concert." More relevant to this context, it can refer to all the ways that we respond when the demands of our work don't allow us to easily default to our preferred behaviors. And these responses, according to William Pannapacker, can hurt us in the long run. He asserts that "[f]or many introverts, being forced to conform to a culture of extroversion has cost them their health, their personal lives, and their sense of integrity and authenticity." It is this final element, a sense of integrity and authenticity, that I am interested in preserving.

But before I start, I want to clearly define terms that will be used for the duration of this section.

I have referenced several times previously in this volume, and will continue to reference, the work of Marti Olson Laney. She stands beside Susan Cain as a significant authority in the research of introversion, and has dedicated a great deal of her life to understanding and deconstructing the causes and effects of temperament differences. She has several books on the topic, all of which are listed in the "On the Shoulders of Giants" section at the end of this book. So with all that said, I'm aware of how audacious it would be to disagree with her on something. But get ready, because it's happening.

At the conclusion of Laney's seminal work *The Introvert Advantage*, she includes a chapter on "extroverting" in the world. It features tips on how to do things like start conversations, share ideas, sustain eye contact, and the like. While I agree with all the advice that was given, I do disagree on one element of the discussion: that any of these things are "extroverting". Being able to connect with individuals is a fundamental human need. In the absence of these connections we would not be "antisocial", or not wanting the company of others, but asocial, or avoiding social interaction. Frankly, I don't find that to be true of most introverts. Most introverts enjoy and appreciate interacting with others; they just prefer a certain set of circumstances to do so easily. And that is the point that I wish to drive home above any other in this section:

Masking introversion is not faking the ability to be social without bounds. Rather, it is the appearance that such behavior is easy.

See the difference? In the former mindset, the emphasis is placed on being able to perform admittedly challenging tasks at all, where the latter places emphasis on the ability to do so *without the appearance of it being difficult*. And it is, at times, difficult.

Laney cites three dimensions of temperament, the reactions to which can distinguish a more introverted individual from a more extroverted one: **energy source**, **response to stimulation**, and **depth versus breadth**. I will use those three dimensions to frame my discussion on the masking of introversion. I will also address some of the consequences of masking, using examples from friends and colleagues to illustrate points.

The Mask of Energy

Think about the last time you were away from home, phone in hand but in need of a charger. As your device's battery life dwindled, chances are you felt increasingly uncomfortable, perhaps pleading with friends to help you find a charger and an outlet, perhaps preparing for a moment where your device would finally give up, and trying to adapt to the remainder of an evening with no power. That scenario is surprisingly similar to the energy management of an introvert in more challenging social situations.

Like a fully charged cellphone, laptop, or tablet, we all have a finite amount of energy with which we start a day, scenario, or individual interaction. The difference is how the outside world affects that energy store. For extroverts, typical interactions such as conversations with acquaintances and exchanges with strangers serve as, to borrow terminology from the world of *Super Mario Brothers,* a "power up" button of sorts, allowing them to grow in energy as Mario or Luigi would when they found a star amidst the bricks. They get faster, louder, and more energetic. But for introverts, those interactions are more like Goombas- the side shuffling mushroom enemies of Mario and Luigi. When they encounter Goombas, they can still function for a time, but they lose some of their shine. They literally grow smaller. And, given enough exposure to the Goombas, they run out of energy completely. So the challenge for introverts, then, is to wear a mask of energy where it would normally actually be de-energizing, to behave as though one had encountered a star instead of a Goomba.

To make this example live in the context of our work, I'll use a time of year that is a constant challenge for the introverted hearts among us- new student orientation. My first year of orientation at a small school had me wearing several more hats than I was accustomed to. The result? Lots of human interaction and very little time to plug my charger in, even for a few minutes. Even the off days were crowded with meetings that had to be postponed as staff members worked with our incoming students.

Meeting all of our new students and their parents was enjoyable for the ability to see the faces I'd be working with in the fall. However, it was not enjoyable in the sense that these interactions necessarily occurred in short bursts grouped closely together. As days wore on, and I was pulled to assist with more and more tasks that favored short interactions over long periods, the smiling face I wear in times of high stimulation was harder and harder to put on. Remember: it's not whether or not I can do these sorts of tasks, *but whether or not they appear easy*. Heidi, a residence life professional, shared a story about a staff retreat that describes well how being in that difficult spot can feel:

> We stayed at a lodge where there were 3-4 people per room and no alone time for three days (over a weekend after a full week of RA training and evening in halls). Immediately upon returning to campus, professional staff were expected to dive into a work day/ week (we got back on a Monday) [...] After the first day with no alone time with exception of showering, I was spent and could feel myself getting anxious and overwhelmed by all the time around people. When I finally got a little quiet time that Monday evening, it felt like I could breathe again, and I felt the tension inside me that was building throughout the retreat melt away.

These moments are part of the job and we all have to leave our comfort zone, so just as Heidi did, I endured. But as my fellow introverts know from experience, sustained interactions of the variety we experience during orientation season can be damaging.

How damaging can this deprival from "recharge time" be? Damaging enough to cause stress earaches. That's right, I was tense enough from the lack of time to relax and recollect that I clenched my teeth until my ears hurt. It wasn't until the weekend, when I sequestered myself with the assumption that I had a double ear infection that my jaw relaxed enough for my pain to go away. So while temperament is considered a preference, it can have physical effects if the preference is not sufficiently heeded.

Interestingly enough, my most calm moments of my orientation days came when I had the chance to meet with commuter students. Because they are a relatively small percentage of our population, and an even smaller percentage of our first year students, my sessions with that group had at most twenty students. My discomfort and physical tension melted away as I led them on a tour around campus, informing them of their resources on campus. While it wasn't particularly deep conversation unto itself, it was centered on a topic about which I have a great deal of knowledge, and the ability to talk in a small group on a topic of interest gave me the most rejuvenation that schedule was able to afford.

What does a mask of energy look like in a scenario like this?

Returning to the analogy of a mobile device for a moment, a mask can take the form of what is commonly referred to as "airplane mode" or "game mode". This mode of operation for a mobile device allows it to perform functions that don't require connectivity, while maintaining the appearance of being fully functioning. For humans, airplane mode means engaging in these exchanges superficially. If you've ever had to fake attentiveness in a boring lecture or through a particularly boring conversation, you know precisely what I mean. All the social cues are there- seeming eye contact, supportive affirmations like "mm-hmm" and "oh yeah, I feel ya there"- but the mind have moved elsewhere. It has shut down to conserve energy, directed its stores inward to jumpstart a flagging system.

My airplane mode switch turns on most often at the tail end of departmental of divisional meetings, when "report-outs" are most common. The meat of the meeting is captivating for introverts, who like to make connections between the tasks of departments and their own projects. Lists of information don't captivate in the same way. So while I do pay attention and take note of relevant dates and action items, I allow my mind and heart to wander, conserving power for later tasks and interactions.

But while this manner of operation has no damaging effect on a mobile phone (at least over time) it can have a lasting effect on introverts. When we succumb to the urge to go through our daily interactions in airplane mode, we do gain some minimal conservation of energy. But we trade in something many introverts value far more highly than that: authenticity. The nature of introversion lends many with this temperament to extraordinary listening skills. Nuances in conversation that could be glossed over by extroverts, who tend to be less attentive to nonverbal cues, are keenly picked up on by the more inwardly focused introvert. So when we actively choose to forgo use of this rare gift, we feel badly about it. What's more, we're likely to hold on to those bad feelings, ruminating on them later, even after the threat of being uncovered as a "faker" has passed. So the energy conservation that is has given to us in the short run is expended later on, in the form of lamenting our lack of listening skills.

Deep talks of the variety that introverts truly enjoy came at the end of the commuter session I mentioned earlier, when the tour concluded and we were able to talk closely as a group. Orientation leaders who had commuted or are preparing to commute shared their experiences, and new students chimed in to ask questions or voice concerns. These interactions had a way of energizing me after an hour of flitting about campus, accompanied by a rapidly draining battery and the oppressive heat of Boston in June. While I was exhausted, this was not the time to switch into airplane mode; the well being of a group of students was at stake, and I wanted to really hear their challenges. I'm glad I didn't "shut it down", because the energy of these discussions sustained me for the remainder of my long day. Deep conversations about meaningful topics are the introvert's "power-up" stars, and I found those stars in the smallest of my orientation sessions.

The Mask of Normal Stimulation

Don't make this one weird. As I've said many times before, the operative term with introverts is *overly stimulated*. However, we don't live in the sort of society where it's normal or acceptable to excuse oneself because the energy in the room has become too much. So just as love means never having to say you're sorry, introversion can sometimes mean not getting to say "No, thank you." To compare it to a more common phenomenon, think about being tickled. It may be something that you don't really mind in short bursts. But even in your enjoyment of it, it can be uncomfortable. And it all of a sudden shifts and becomes uncomfortable. Once one hits that point, you can stand it no longer. The quick shift from enjoying being tickled, to needing it to stop immediately, is a physical manifestation of overstimulation. For introverts, some forms of socializing or social environments are like a tickling fit waiting to be abruptly halted.

Think about the afternoon before a major event in your office, or the Friday before a long weekend of duty, or the eve of a major deadline for prospective student application submissions. Kelley S. sees these days often:

The most challenging situations for me at work are days with several hours of meetings coupled with a high volume of student and staff needs. My office is located in an area such that students and staff always have access to me (they do not need to set up an appointment with me in advance and there is not a "front line" staff member to help manage interruptions.) These tend to be the days without any re-charging time or quiet time and I am constantly giving myself pep talks when it seems the revolving door does not stop moving.

But I learned in talking to friends as I wrote this book, it can always be worse. Consider the story my friend Emily M. shared about one of the most highly charged activities one can partake in -- the flash mob:

> At orientation one summer, we (being the Division) decided to plan a flash mob for one of the orientation sessions. Everyone was participating, and I wanted to be included. I didn't want someone to think I was a poor

sport or wasn't a team player, so I agreed to be a part of the flash mob.

Any of these situations can invite a frenzied environment. In fact, I'm sitting in one right now. As I write this, students have been in and out of my office to borrow the departmental credit card, get information about their newly recognized organizations, and pick up their reserved hockey tickets. There's a lot going on in here. But I have to be careful to not let that overstimulation show through *too* much. Comparatively, my coworker Kelly on the other side of the wall thrives from the traffic that similarly passes through her office. As I grow more and more tired from the short but fairly straightforward conversations I've engaged in today, she gets more and more energized from the same actions. Neither reaction is bad, they're simply different.

Emily's reaction to the madness of the flash mob was likely just what I would have experienced in the same situation. She recalls, "I made it to the first practice session. And froze. If I froze in front of 30 people, what on earth was I going to do in front of 250 people?"

What does the mask of normal stimulation look like?

So the mask of normal stimulation comes in acting as though I expect each knock on the door, and that it isn't difficult for me to go through the day with the knowledge that someone could come at any time. Yes, I make and keep appointments, but drop-ins are an inevitability in my work and I have to steel myself for their impending arrival. Interestingly enough, some of the same strategies that work to mask the overstimulation are the ones that help mask the energy drops we just discussed. As I continue to write this, my email notifications have been turned off, my instant messaging shut down, and my phone is literally on airplane mode. Sometimes managing being overstimulated means taking away some of the other potential distractions or interruptions. Along with those procedural shifts are an ever-constant shift of mindset about the nature of my work. As I've written previously, these things like phones, email alerts, and the beeps of an instant messenger are the distractions- not students:

> Yes, there are tasks that can be more easily completed when we are unfettered by appointments, meetings, and questions from students who pop in. But students aren't distractions, and they aren't interruptions. They are the reason that we do what we do. They are assets. They keep us from having "hobbies" of editing manuals, completing paperwork, and developing training and educational opportunities. And I don't know about all of you, but when I list my hobbies, I have not once ever listed these things.

Further, in a somewhat crass but absolutely correct way, "a customer [or student] is really just a little bundle of future cash flow [or another form of capital] with a memory. And this future cash flow [or other form of capital] will increase or decrease based on how the customer remembers being treated, today." That is to say, a student's experience is affected positively or negatively based on how we treat him or her. How do you greet a student who comes in without an appointment? Do you try to multitask? Do you turn off your monitor to focus your attention? Do you turn him or her away, asking instead for a formally scheduled meeting? I know that this goes into issues of "how available do we want to be?" or "how can we set boundaries and encourage the following of procedure?". That's not what I'm talking about here; what I'm referring to is an overall spirit of reception and treatment of students as the reason we work, not an impediment to it.

So as important as having the temporal capital to manage our days is essential (a goal that I achieve by having several hours at the end of the week where I am in the office working on tasks but do not make appointments or accept walk-ins), it is equally important to have the mental and emotional capital to understand that elements of our job that are difficult, are still part of our job. We do certain things that are against our nature, as Susan Cain has put it, in service to what we do. As Kelley alluded to in her account of her busiest days, we sometimes have to talk ourselves into our best work. And if we really can't do them, Emily says, sometimes its best to just opt out and accept that our talents will have to be utilized in other ways:

> I think that in that moment I learned a powerful lesson. It was better for me to take ownership of my personality style and where I draw my energy from than to back out because I committed in an effort to "fit in." And you know what- when the flash mob came up again the following year and I confidently (and graciously) passed on the opportunity, it wasn't questioned because learning to see my introversion as a strength allowed others to see it as a strength as well.

The Mask of Breadth

Returning to the example of orientation season for

just a moment, what specific elements of orientation can illustrate this difference in approach? One notorious way in which introverts and extroverts differ in their approaches to socialization comes in the form of small talk. Small talk affords extroverts the opportunity to talk to someone new, but on a surface level. The burden of getting to know someone is small, because you may never encounter this person again. To many extroverts (remember, not all, for shy extroverts do exist!) this is a relatively simple enterprise. They find a commonality and can typically jump into a conversation with ease. As the conversation develops, you can see the extrovert's eyes shine with the energy of discovering a star worth a thousand points. Meeting new students and their parents at orientation is a great example of this. Extroverts pull sustenance from these brief exchanges, appreciating that this student or that family will look familiar later in the day or even in the fall. These fragments of conversation help them "power up".

Conversely, the introvert sees a pair of Goombas in the prospect of small talk. Julia F., a career services professional says it quite well as she voices one of the biggest challenges to her nature at work:

> I would say the most challenging situation I face in my work in networking with employers at our career fairs. Specifically lunchtime, I have had to be "On" all day and all I want to do is sit with people I know and eat my University catered lunch. BUT as a member of the team we are encouraged to sit with employers and make small talk. I really hate small talk, I feel like I can only think of the most awkward things to say, and run out of topics before I finish my salad.

Julia's feelings about small talk and the difficulties with making it are common of introverts, for two reasons. First, the energy it takes to remove oneself from the rich inner world he or she typically inhabits "shrinks" the individual a bit. Laurie Helgoe, the author of Introvert Power, says it almost exactly this way:

> Introverts do not hate small talk because we hate people. We hate small talk because of the barrier it creates between people. We want less -- and more: less talk, more

understanding. [...] We are a mix of a lot of things, but conversation generally *reduces* us. (Emphasis added)

Making that first contact is difficult enough, because it requires a shift from the default mindset of ideas and concepts, to one of people. The second Goomba in the scenario is resisting the urge to create an exchange that values depth over breadth. I'll speak more about this in a later chapter, but will speak briefly on the issue here. The type of conversation that introverts thrive in is deep and compelling, significant and meaningful. It allows for seemingly endless richness of debate and expression. But sometimes, this depth of conversation is neither appropriate nor possible. We would likely make that parent stopping at an information table, or student meeting us during a social event, uncomfortable if we tried to delve into our worldview on a topic during a five-minute exchange. Further, according to Brené Brown, this type of vulnerability cannot be forced without a foundation and connection that likely will not be made in that period. So we're left in a situation in which we can do little but watch the Goomba head toward us, sensing the imminence of an energy drop.

What does a mask of breadth look like?

You may have guessed from our earlier discussion of masks for energy and normal stimulation- masking the discomfort of interest in broad or surface discussion involves "faking" many of the cues that would be real in a more engaging or deep conversation. Nonverbal signals of rapt attention, like nodding to signify attention and audibles of understanding, are constantly at hand in the social arsenal of the introvert.

However, there are also ways to create depth in situations that normally call for surface interactions. To eliminate the need for a mask of breadth, create opportunities for broad activities to take on some depth. Transform these brief interactions from organized small talk, to something more meaningful and memorable. For example, when selecting an icebreaker, choose ones that go beyond surface characteristics- ask about favorite childhood toys or origins of participants' names. These activities serve their intended purpose (helping students or staff get to know one another) while keeping an "energizing" activity from being draining to, statistically, a significant portion of the group. Similarly, meetings with students to discuss policy or procedure could be infused with additional conversation about their experiences and thoughts. While this might seem like common sense, we can sometimes get swept up in the momentum of our work and truncate human interaction in hopes of finding energy afterward, in solitude. Resist this urge. Find that energy from your students and colleagues- they can provide it with rich and meaningful conversation.

The Introvert Hangover

When speaking about temperament, a great deal of discussion surrounds what introverts need to truly be at their best. Time to recharge, a permitted slower pace, and the opportunity to express oneself in writing are all ways that introverts stay at their best. But these statements don't address one thing: what happens if introverts don't have these things? What does an introvert at less than his or her best look like?

As with many other questions I had in crafting this book, I took to the Internet to ask my friends and colleagues:

"[M]any I's mentioned they need time to recharge to be their best. What happens if you don't get that time?"

Here is a sampling of the answers I received:

> *"[I] get short with folks and have no time for nonsense. Ick. I've found other ways of coping, but that's my reaction..."* (Gwen)

Gwen's sentiment about getting short with people was a common thread I noted as responses to my question rolled in. Heidi T. was one of those who agreed, saying, "Small annoyances become a bigger deal than necessary." Other words that echoed in the answers I received: "cranky", "irritable", and "unreasonable".

> *"I call it the introvert hangover - I get irritable and lose focus if I go too long without quiet time"* (Chris)

Chris's response was one that resonated with several people, and is so indicative of the problem at hand. A hangover from alcohol or sugar (and yes, a sugar hangover is real) comes from the consumption of an excess amount of something that, in appropriate amounts, has few ill effects. But after we reach a threshold that our body can handle, we start to feel ill. The introvert hangover is our body's response to excess- irritability, short temperedness, and a loss of focus. When we look back on some of the negative characteristics associated with introversion- assumptions of judgment, self-centeredness, and aloofness - one starts to wonder if these conclusions were drawn from introverts who were, as Chris says, hungover. These characteristics generally aren't true from a "fully charged" introvert, but could certainly be mistakenly assumed of an introvert in dire need of a recharge.

In addition to affecting our relationships with others, burnout from "over-extroversion" could affect our relationships with ourselves, as one answer notes:

> *"I am unable to focus on anything, make tons of mistakes, miss details, and can't get in touch with my F." (Sue)*

When Sue refers to her "F", she speaks to the Feeling portion of her Myers-Briggs personality type. While this book strives to address introversion beyond its MBTI definition, this is an important point to bring up. The Feeling parameter of the MBTI affects, among other things, our ability to empathize with others and desire to address the needs of others. Although not all introverts are of the Feeling variety, those who are will not be able to constructively or skillfully work well with others if they cannot channel their Feeling side. So if given the opportunity to create an environment where people must work together harmoniously, be sure that it is a place where introverts have time to recharge and reach their full potential. The dynamic of the group will suffer noticeably if this time is not provided.

After a recent "extrovert bender" during a busy time at work, I tried to look through bleary and tired eyes at what I must have looked like to those around me. When I really think about it, the myths mentioned in the first three chapters truly held up. I was silent in nearly all moments where I didn't have to speak. I ached for a quiet moment to spend by myself and visibly bristled when those moments of solitude were interrupted. I surely seemed as though I wanted to separate myself from the projects altogether. And most importantly, there wasn't a mask in the world I could have worn to hide those facts. My energy reserves were simply too low to hide it all.

Our three myths, in that moment of extreme exhaustion and a nearly dead battery, held up. But the reason I still hold them up as myths is because they are not *always* true. They are not our "factory setting", as it were. Only when truly pushed to our limit, and our energy stores are nearing their complete depletion, will you see these qualities in us. In the sections that follow, as I offer tips on how to navigate these environments based on your role, I hope to offer a bit of guidance on what to do if you need to function in this environment while "hungover", so to speak.

Sometimes, the mask that we put on is essential to our survival. But masks aren't sustainable for long periods. It gets hot under there. It's itchy and it gets hard to breathe. And no matter how long you wear them, they don't become a part of you. So how can you move from feeling the need to wear a mask, to being able to come out of proverbial hiding? The chapters that follow will give you some guidance, paired with the testimony of introverts and extroverts, that will allow you to show your best introverted face to the office, your students, and the world around you.

CHAPTER FIVE
The Introverted Interviewee

As we've seen by this point, there are many benefits to be seen by having introverts in our companies on our campuses. They are deliberative and thorough, typically considerate and tactful. But William Pannapacker, in his wonderful *Chronicle* article "Screening Out the Introverts" (a wonderful read that I highly recommend for anyone interested in how students view temperament), encapsulates well the concerns that introverts should raise about interview processes in student affairs:

> When there are so many job candidates with excellent written credentials, 'fit' and personality take on a magnified importance. One could hardly devise a more brutal process for disadvantaged introverts than the two-day, on-campus interview- involving multiple high-stakes meetings with important strangers, a public lecture, and a teaching demonstration, all in an unfamiliar location with little or no time to recharge between events.

For me, Pannapacker's detailed account of what the interview process typically entails was exhausting to *read*, let alone live during each of my job searches. Preparing to be away from home for a sometimes uncertain amount of time (travel delays do happen, and they further agitate the already overstimulated psyche of many whom they befall), meeting and interacting with people you don't know or don't know well, and participating in a whirlwind schedule of events with little to no time to collect yourself in between can all weigh heavily on the introvert. Pannapacker asks later in his article, "I wonder how those who tend toward introversion [...] have coped with these demands. And what can institutions do to serve their needs more effectively?" If you're not sure, consider how you were interviewed for your most recent position.

I would place good money on the fact that it was at least a half-day process (at the most extreme, two full days!) in which you were paraded around a campus to meet with several campus constituencies, asked several questions, and given little time to recollect yourself in between. As it happens, this system works wonders for the energy level of extroverts. In the presence of people, being able to talk out their thoughts, and little idle time, extroverts thrive. But if this is the extrovert equivalent of plugging a phone into a charger, it is the introvert equivalent of trying to play six games on that phone at one time. Power is quickly drained, and at a time where power is needed the most. Is this any way to introduce new people to our environment? But I'll save further thoughts on that process, as well as a few alternatives, for later.

I took to my friends and colleagues to address Pannapacker's first question. Jessi's response was a very interesting one, and spoke about an element of the job search that comes well before the interview- the resume and cover letter that hopefully will get one's foot in the door for an interview:

> [I]t takes a long time to write/update my cover letter/resume because I feel like I'm not bragging enough, but am afraid to talk to highly of myself for fear it will be seen as boastfulness or making myself out to be more than I am. I finally reached out to a couple people [...] because I knew my cover letter was junk, but it was difficult because part of my introversion is based in a world where it's

easier to do [things] myself than interact with others or expose myself to criticism.

Jessi highlights two significant hallmarks of introverts in her response. The first is a tendency to downplay the positive, especially as it pertains to themselves. While many introverts express themselves better in writing than they do via the spoken word (likely because of the ability to work in an asynchronous fashion), many have trouble with the self-promotion that is so encouraged in the job search process. Their tendency to internalize processes and say little unless it's truly meaningful makes bragging feel disingenuous. Moreover, their attentive and observant nature leads them to pay close attention to the good work of others. As such, they are accustomed to their work speaking for them, and not having to supplement it with their own words.

A second struggle for introverts is being able to summon the courage and humility to reach out and accept criticism, however constructive it may be. An inward focus means introverts are accustomed to hearing criticism...from themselves. So focusing attention outward and opening ourselves to criticism from others is difficult. We know how to react when our inner voices ask questions we may not be prepared to answer, but what do we do when someone else voices those questions?

However, just as has been a running theme in this book, Jessi's ability to open up beyond her comfort zone led her to challenge these two struggles in the pursuit of success. Another hallmark of the introverted mind is perfectionism, a quality likely fueled by our propensity to turn thoughts over and over in our minds until they have reached near perfection. In the end, that desire for perfection occasionally overwhelms the desire to keep our work private, and we must share to ensure success.

There are many other ways that the natural tendencies of introverts can help the job search process. If you are an introvert preparing to embark on, or are currently in the midst of, a job search, some of these tips may help. And if you are seeking new employees, some of this information may help you understand the mindset of any introverts you may encounter in the process.

While Searching For Positions

Know your limits. Jeff P., currently at the Ohio State University, used his knowledge of his temperament as he sought out specific opportunities. "I'm introverted by nature, so I'm intentional about what I apply for," he said when asked about his strategies for the search. Go into your job search with a clear list of what you need from a position, and with an equally detailed list of tasks or scenarios that will not work for you. Try to see the potential for an introvert hangover in your future roles, carefully considering how often this position could bring you to that crucial point. As an example, my particular brand of introversion is ill suited for live-on work. I learned that during my time in residence life, and it was confirmed after a summer of doing live-on student activities work. It would have been a poor decision for me to pursue live-on work, because its challenges are so contrary to my nature. I would have done the work poorly and been unhappy.

Be steadfast in determining your needs and non-negotiables up front, and deviate from them only if you have other equally pressing constraints (such as a severely depressed job market, considerable geographic constraints, or other absolute nonnegotiable circumstances).

Talk to your friends and colleagues. The beauty of the small field in which we work is that connections between colleagues and institutions are quite common. If you can make a connection with someone who works in an office or at an institution that you're interested in, find a way to organically make a connection with him or her and discuss what the climate of your potential new workplace is like. Jessi mentioned the inertia struggle that many introverts feel as they contemplate a change when she noted, "I'm terrified to leave the familiarity of my current situation, and I need to know I'm going to a good fit."

She's far from alone in this fear- *what if I get to my next location and hate it? What if I end up not finding what I was looking for?* Analysis paralysis is a common demon for introverts, and it is especially pronounced during times of decision-making. But with perspective about your prospective new environment, it is easier to start contemplating different circumstances.

Research, research, research. It plays to the

strengths of introverts to focus deeply on areas of interest. If your future place of employment is the topic of your research, it will only help you in the process. Use all the resources at your disposal to learn about your prospective institution. Dive into learning about your potential future school with the same exuberance that a prospective student would. Find local press about the institution to learn more about their relationship with the community. See if you can find the student newspaper to learn about what issues are of importance to the students. And count on your networks to help you identify current and former employees. As we all know, our field is small; enlist the social butterflies and the superconnectors in your network to help you find those you could be working with. Just as doing the required reading and homework will spell success for a college course, channeling your likely enjoyment of research as an introvert could spell success for your search.

In Written Materials

In a May 2013 post on my blog, I wrote about my reaction to a Chronicle article entitled "Are You Too Good To Be Recognized?" A few excerpts are below, discussing common problems that happen when introverts are asked to speak about themselves.

To sum up, it discusses how some who exhibit quiet or humble leadership don't get recognized because they don't speak up for themselves, and how some of those quiet leaders miss recognition opportunities because it is assumed by nominators that someone else will speak up for the person. I experienced the latter firsthand in a conversation with my director the other day. He was lamenting the lack of a leadership award nomination for our SGA president, who had served dutifully for several years with the board. Of the staff in our office, he has worked with her the most closely. But when I asked if he had nominated her, he shook his head and admitted he hadn't. This fell true to form with an example given in the story: a young woman given an award in her senior year was awarded it with the remark, "You must have several of these." But she didn't. So many people assumed that someone else would recognize her, that NO ONE recognized her.

[...] Whatever the reason, be it temperament or culture, some simply won't speak up to be recognized, even if others might feel that they deserve it. So how is this tension to be resolved? I will not claim to be an authority on the matter, but I have a few ideas.

Acknowledge it. Too many contemporary practices of career counseling and office etiquette emphasize the dominant culture's request to speak up for oneself, and "toot the proverbial horn". But alternatives need to be recognized. Not everyone plays that instrument (hence the title of this post). For whatever reason, some simply aren't built that way. Don't treat it as odd or problematic; acknowledge it for what it is.

Give credit where credit is due. Although I am not a self-promoter (it doesn't come naturally to me), I do acknowledge good work where I see it. I pride myself on being a prompt gratitude giver, and I like to give it in a way that is comfortable for me and lasting for the person- thank you notes. It's not everyone's style, but I would never want anyone to think I didn't appreciate what he or she did for me.

Why is this post relevant to the discussion at hand? The written materials of an application are your opportunity to speak about yourself in glowing terms, being specific about the quantifiable measures of your success and making those who need to know about your accomplishments, aware. I will be the first to admit, this is not an easy process. But Susan Cain said something wonderful when I saw her at an in-store book discussion: sometimes the things that are difficult or unnatural, we are willing to do in service to something we care about. Assuming your job is something that you care about, the temporary push to self-promote could be a little easier to endure.

While Interviewing

Channel your enthusiasm for the prospective role. Jessica P., a recent graduate currently in her search, made an excellent point about any job seeker: "[W]hen I'm excited about something I usually go for it." Introverts get excited, but their excitement looks a little different from that of an extrovert. Introverts who are excited by the prospect of a position or its duties should channel that energy and convey it strategically over the course of the interview. Judge, Bono, Iles, and Gerhardt (2002) found in their studies that "extroverted employees are significantly more likely to (1) emerge as leaders in selection and promotion decisions, and (2) be perceived as effective by both supervisors and subordinates."

With this in mind, it will be all the more important to reveal your excitement as the situation or topic of conversation calls for it. When should you "unleash" it? While you should always be attentive and upbeat about a role in interviews, two main constituencies *need* to see that energy: your prospective staff (immediate coworkers), and students. If you must parcel out your energy over the course of the day, ensure that those two groups see the best and most enthusiastic version of you.

Alternatively, unleash your enthusiasm when speaking to people about elements of the job that most excite you. Because introverts truly come alive when working deeply on projects that excite you, the most advantageous time to express excitement may be when addressing projects that will *give* you the most energy.

Accept breaks when they are offered; create them if needed. The days are long when you are on an interview. You may trudge from room to room in rapid succession without attention to your "battery life," a situation that could spell trouble at an intermediate time. If you sense your proverbial needle is plunging toward "E" and you are headed toward the dreaded introvert hangover, take any breaks that are offered to you to breathe and recharge. If these breaks are not naturally offered, request a bathroom break and make the most of your few moments away. Close your eyes and take a few deep breaths. Even a short moment of solitude can do wonders for your ability to focus and respond naturally. Don't ignore your needs this early in the process; if you do that, it could hinder your portrayal to your potential coworkers. Related to that...

Voice your needs and style. Another thing that must be unleashed during your interview is how your introversion and its associated traits affect your work. When asked questions about your work style and what you need to be successful, do your best to artfully integrate information that will help your prospective coworkers and supervisors learn about how you work best. Should you be offered and accept the position, you will have to work in conditions discussed in the interview. Make sure those conversations include frank and open talk about a need for advance notice to get things done, time to decompress, and the ability to create and maintain an environment that allows for necessary recharging.

After Interviewing

Follow up thoughtfully in writing. I am an avowed proponent of a well-written thank you card sent swiftly after an interview. This is both an important way to show gratitude for their consideration, and a wonderful opportunity to inject details or pose questions that you recall from the interesting conversations that you had with others over the course of the interview day. Use the introverted propensity to remember names and small details as you compose these notes; your thorough and thoughtful nature will be appreciated here.

I also strongly recommend ensuring that thoughtful thank you notes are written to any students you meet over the course of your interview process.

Reference the conversations that you had with them, wish them luck in their academic endeavors, and show genuine interest in their experience. Care for the students you work with is essential to the work that we do; what better place to display it than in a note addressed to them?

Move forward. I recognize how difficult this tip will be to take, but I'm listing it anyway. Introversion lends itself well to rumination, even mild forms of obsession, in the days and weeks following an interview. But this intense focus on something that has already happened can detract success in interim endeavors; this can be particularly dangerous if you are still working in another role! Make an agreement with yourself to ruminate about the process for a finite amount of time after your interview, and then refocus yourself on other things.

Interviews are, in their purest form, a performance. They are a finite amount of time when you get to put your best foot forward, speak passionately about something you're (hopefully) excited about, and are typically conducted without interruption. In many ways, interviews take place under the same circumstances as public speaking engagements do. It may help you to review the steps in Chapter Two about public speaking. Preparation, enthusiasm and excitement are all great skills to harness as you pursue an opportunity to continue your life's work. If Julia Roberts and Will Ferrell can do it, so can you!

INsights

- ⇒ Take advantage of the fact that your written materials may be the strongest opportunity to express who you are to hiring authorities. Infuse stories of how you handle situations, your thoughts on challenges you may encounter, and how you're a wonderful fit for the position in question, in your resume and cover letter.
- ⇒ Make time for yourself in the days leading up to your interview! You wouldn't leave for a road trip without making sure your GPS had access to power, and you shouldn't do the same for yourself either!
- ⇒ As you interview, take notes on things you'd like to follow up on or have more questions

about, and use these notes to inform and fill in your thank you correspondence. Being attentive and wanting to talk more is highly desirable, and those meaty displays of appreciation beat a generic "thank you" most days of the week.

⇒ *For more information on how to operationalize this knowledge when interviewing students, please see the Guide for Interviewing the Introvert at the end of this book, after the References.*

CHAPTER SIX
The Introverted Employee

"You're an introvert? I never would have guessed that!"

I can't tell you how many times my friends and family have uttered that exact phrase and as I researched this book, spoke with colleagues about my interests, and solicited input. When pushed to explain that statement, the response generally boiled down to one of the following statements:

"But you're so good with people!"
"But you're a great public speaker!"
"But you're around people all day!"

I don't say that to share the praise that I received from those around me, I promise! The reason I share these observations is because these are qualities most of society equates with extroversion. As a corollary, this means that most people expect introverts to cower in the face of an audience, or shy away from people all together. I'm honestly not fully clear on where this cave-dwelling, trembling-leaf perception of introversion came from, but I can hazard a guess that traces all the way back to the origin of the study of temperament. Interestingly enough, it was a fight amongst men that led to all these negative stereotypes of introversion.

Freud, Jung, and The Root of Misconception

Carl Jung developed his initial metric of temperament during his time as an associate of Sigmund Freud. He characterized those who had an internal focus, toward ideas and concepts, as "introverts". This way of being was one that he saw in himself, as well as in another protégée of Freud's, Alfred Adler. The opposite of his introversion was extroversion, a focus outward toward the world and the people in it. This way of being is one that he attributed to Freud, his mentor and collaborator. Relations between Freud and his two younger colleagues grew strained as their research interests shifted; Jung and Adler wished to explore other elements of their careers, and this angered Freud. How angry was he? Angry enough to pepper his research findings on temperament to deceive the world for nearly one hundred years. That's right, characterizations of introverts in Freud's research as "neurotic", "self-centered", and "anti-social" are actually personal attacks on Jung and Adler, not accurate portrayals of their actual nature or the actual nature of introverts. Why have they persisted for so long, you may ask? Perhaps, a better question would be "would you be willing to say Sigmund Freud is wrong?" As it happens, not many were…until fairly recently.

This understanding of introversion, despite efforts to debunk it, does persist in fields where introversion seems contrary to the ideal for the profession. Politics and entertainment often equate garrulousness, charm, and even good humor with extroversion, leaving quieter individuals feeling left behind. If the measure of values can be taken from how we treat the next generation, then our preparation of student leaders can be another way in which we treat extroversion as an ideal, indeed even a sole route to success. Which students are most likely to ascend to leadership positions, if staff are selecting? Those students who absolutely dazzle us. Those who have well prepared and effortless responses to our painstakingly crafted interview questions. Those who can easily work in a group. Those who match (or at times exceed) the expectations of what they put on paper in the application stage.

The reason I qualify this with staff selection is that I've seen considerably more diversity in student-selected leadership candidates where temperament is concerned. My best guess as to why this happens is that, as students grow more comfortable with one another, their temperament in that group becomes more collegial, and the true merits of that individual shine through. While it is appreciated that selection committees for student leaders often include representatives from all over campus, this often invites people to the table that don't know students well enough to overcome their presentation of temperament, thus excluding solid but quiet leaders from important roles and learning opportunities.

I am pleased, however, to see that the tide is turning somewhat on this. Where we used to look on polished and effortless leaders with blind adoration, I have seen this mentality challenged more and more in recent years. Increased importance of what social psychologist Adam Grant calls "powerless communication" allows us to see imperfection in speech or presentation (something that introverts are often prone to) as endearing and non-threatening, rather than weak or incompetent. Many environments are now seeing the merit of allowing both to exist alongside one another. Thank goodness for that!

If I had to make a cursory guess at which functional areas of student affairs most people would classify as inherently extroverted or introverted, the breakdown would look something like this (note that where these departments may fall at your institution may vary):

Extroverted: new student orientation, housing and residence life, student activities, admissions, development and alumni relations, multicultural programs, athletics, leadership education, and fraternity and sorority life
Introverted: academic advising, financial aid, career services, counseling services, instructional technology, and human resources

But here's the trouble with making these distinctions at all: it invites the assumption that those in those areas *have* to be one way over another. But despite some physiological differences that distinguish introverts from extroverts, we are all capable of all the qualities that these positions require. That said, some elements of those positions may be easier than others.

When it comes to the mask of energy that introverts occasionally have to slip on, there is a great deal of attention paid to the times when too little energy remains to be effective. Indeed, that is a situation that introverts find themselves in often. However, there is a less commonly known energy imbalance that introverts are also vulnerable to, and it pertains to precisely that- *vulnerability*. Kristen voiced her thoughts on this energy imbalance well, as it pertains to presenting at orientation:

> For the past several years, I have had to present at orientations – whether it was on sexual assault and healthy relationships or student housing – and usually I have had to present more than once per orientation. In addition, the past few years a small talk element has been added to the duties of directors at orientation – one of my least favorite things in the world. It used to be that orientation was just a Saturday morning event at my current institution, and as much as I hated coming in on a Saturday morning, I'm not going to lie that I very much appreciated not having to work the afternoons it occurred. When we changed to a weekday orientation, more than once I remarked how difficult it was for me to work in the afternoons because of all the energy required for me to do well at orientations and gotten a strange look.

Kristen followed this testimony with the observation, "I guess people don't understand introverts here that well." But this misunderstanding is one that crops up often, not just at her institution. And while the lack of energy appears to be the most frustrating element of this scenario, this feeling of being misunderstood can be equally (or even more) damaging.

The Introverted Advisor
Though required competencies for student affairs professionals may vary widely across functional areas, advising is one that the overwhelming majority of us will undertake at some point in our careers. According to Patrick Love, "Advising may be the universal task in student affairs, because it exists at the foundation of much of the work we do [...] Advising is the out-of-class activity provided to all students and, therefore, in many cases may be the only opportunity for a student to develop a personal link outside the institution." Love goes on to further explain the purpose of the advising function:

> Advising is not merely providing advice.

> Providing advice is a unidirectional relationship in which a person who "knows better" tells another person what to do. Advising is a helping relationship between two people and a dynamic process of mutual discover and self-determination [...] While the advisor may indeed have more knowledge and experience than the advisee and be aware of the "bigger picture," the goal of advising is to generate learning, growth, and self-determination, in addition to sharing information, opinion, and one's accumulated wisdom.

Introverts, by their very nature, are well equipped to serve in the advising role. Advising allows them to do many things that were previously discussed in the Myths chapters- share knowledge on a topic that they are deeply invested in and know a great deal about, while also creating and sustaining a one-on-one conversation or relationship with a student. Introverts are naturally avid and attentive listeners, with a keen ability to make the person they're speaking to feel as though they're being heard and understood. And because they speak carefully, the information shared and advice dispensed is thoughtful and comprehensive. Further, the nature of most advising interactions can create an environment conducive for our introverted students to express themselves without interruption, distraction, or fear of judgment; the time that we devote to our quieter students could, in some instances, be the only prolonged time they get to spend with someone who understands their temperament.

These qualities could also apply well for advisors who work with groups, rather than individuals. Their ability to absorb information and create new connections could be helpful when assisting organizations in troubleshooting a problem, and can be endlessly helpful when building trust with and among students; their ability to sense the mood of a room and at times the underlying causes can help them effectively address issues of group conflict.

If ever there were a function that most required the patience and attentiveness of the introverted mind, it would be advising. When carefully and appropriately executed, the advising relationship can be the most impactful element of many introverted student affairs professionals' work. However, there is a caveat that must be addressed here. Alongside the tendency for introverts to think deeply and listen attentively, is the propensity to internalize thought. When these advising relationships contain sensitive, emotional, or even disturbing information, introverts are more likely to internalize these conversations and their potential effects, a situation that could lead to the aforementioned "introverted hangover." While we are all prone to "taking our work home" at the end of each day, the nature of the introverted brain may make it more likely for them to have work weigh on them; such a burden must be effectively dealt with to prevent burnout or resentment.

If you are an introvert who is committed to a high volume of advising, I strongly encourage you to be aware of the emotional load that your work can create, and to explore constructive ways to "escape from your work" now and again. Be it a hobby, a friend outside of the field to whom you can vent, or even some time away from the office, ensure that you don't allow the nature of your work, and your gift with it, to overtake you emotionally.

Handling Disappointments

Because introversion is an internally focused concept, it necessarily creates a kind of insulation between the individual and the rest of the world. It's difficult to peek out from behind that insulation; it takes a tremendous amount of trust and energy to do so. And in the event that this leap isn't rewarded as we expect, we struggle to recover. Criticism that might roll off the back of less internally critical individuals sticks with us, rumination over how we might salvage a bad situation goes on longer than it would for extroverts.

Take, for example, the student event that our office hosts that draws twenty students instead of two hundred. The proposal we present to our boss that gets declined. The student who shows anger at our enforcement of College or University guidelines. Any or all of these situations are uncomfortable for us as professionals. A gap between our expectations and reality is always difficult to overcome. But for introverts, the chasm between our hopes and a less than fulfilling final result is especially difficult to cope with. Why?

Well, think back to your younger days, to a time when you built a sandcastle. If you never did, think of any children you saw doing it on TV or in a movie. These structures take meticulous planning and a great deal of time to set correctly. Grand plans are made in our heads about them standing the test of time, and exceeding our wildest dreams. Now imagine someone knocked down your castle before you were ready. It could be an angry sibling, a careless passerby, or even nature asserting herself in the form of waves breaking on the shore. It's a crushing blow to feel as though your time and work were wasted, as though your efforts weren't appreciated, as they should have been, and as though your confidence is shaken at the sight of a

crumbling construction.

That feeling can consume an introvert when expectations change or the sting of rejection is felt, particularly to those introverts who are also classified as highly sensitive. But just as there is a great deal of confusion about showing too little interest in social endeavors, there is considerable confusion from extroverts about why these, in their eyes, easily navigable setbacks are felt so deeply by their quieter counterparts. Just as we glorify the virtue of charisma, we also glorify the virtue of resilience. And just as with charisma, the appearance of effortless resilience isn't easy. Here again, the application of our operative phrase for the mask of introversion, *ease*, returns to prominence. Moving on after a disappointment is hard for all of us. But rebounding quickly is even harder for introverts.

So how do we soften the blow of these disappointments in a moment where it may not be possible to fully process them?

Restore equilibrium. For all your efforts to temper your reaction to a disappointment or letdown, it may still take you a moment to return to equilibrium. Take that moment. Trying to suppress it or push it off will only place you further off balance, making you more uncomfortable. If you need to adjourn to the nearest restroom, your car, or some hidden place on campus, do so to regain your composure. There is nothing wrong with feeling an emotion fully; allow yourself to do so, with the aid of the other tips listed here.

Adopt a mantra. A mantra isn't going to fix the deep pain, frustration, embarrassment or shame that you feel in the moment after you're hurt, but it will help you to restore composure until you're in an environment where you can truly allow yourself to feel. This mantra should acknowledge what you're feeling, advise you to momentarily put the feeling away, and reassure you that you will overcome what troubles you. One of my go-to mantras to help divert my frustrations is: *"This is uncomfortable right now. But you know it'll pass. You can do this."* Although it may seem terrifically New Age-y to adopt such a method for getting through the roughest of days, a series of short sentences as simple as that can keep you from the rare but significant outbursts introverts can have when overwhelmed.

Recall triumphs. Because introverts find it so easy to retreat to their own thoughts, they have long memories. But all humans, regardless of temperament, hold bad memories more tightly than good ones. The result, for introverts, can be a loop of bad experiences and disappointments. When you're feeling low or defeated, challenge yourself to recall the good memories. Chances are, you have had positive experiences as often (or more often!) as you've had bad ones. Find the good, and allow those moments to fill your thoughts. Don't discount the lessons that can be learned from your mistakes, but don't take the occurrence of a mistake to mean that you're incapable of success either.

Take to the paper. One of my favorite presidents, and a noted introvert, is Abraham Lincoln. Lincoln was a master of the unsent letter. In *Lincoln on Leadership,* Donald T. Phillips spoke of Lincoln's habit of venting frustration through "extended letters of refutation." Phillips noted that the act itself provided the necessary catharsis; "he felt better for having stated his case but did not want any of his angry or emotional remarks made public." A great gift of the introverted mind is its ability to brilliantly and vividly express itself in writing. In times of frustration, high anxiety, or sadness, carry these feelings to the page. Don't worry about grammar, convention, or wording- just express yourself. The ability to express your feelings without judgment or interruption will likely help you calm down, easing your return to equilibrium. You'd be surprised how rejuvenating and recharging an experience this can be.

In *The Introvert and Extrovert in Love*, Marti Laney expertly details the conundrum that exists when introverts and extroverts need to collaborate: "[...] 'innies' tend to think of 'outies' as intrusive, loud and demanding. Outies, on the other hand, see innies as slow, withholding, and mysterious." She speaks of these attributions in the context of a romantic relationship, but these assumptions are no less true of introverts and extroverts striving to coexist in a work environment.

Who among us hasn't felt overpowered or trampled by an extroverted member of our team, or felt as though his or her contributions to a project were making extroverted members of a team bored or impatient? The truth is, just as in romantic relationships, it takes work to be able to understand and eventually love one another. Teamwork, especially in our profession, isn't going anywhere anytime soon. And with calls to 'play nice' across departments and divisions across campus, it would behoove us all to create an understanding of how we work best. How do we do that? These tips could help you answer that question.

Ask. How will you know how someone works if you don't ask? Waiting for conflict to arise is one way, but it's probably not the best one. Rather, when a committee forms, make learning about one another a priority. Please note: I'm not referring, in this instance to the equally utilized and dreaded icebreaker. I'm referring, instead, to facilitating a dialogue about work styles, motivations, and pet peeves. I've done an exercise with student staff, based on a model published in *How Full Is Your Bucket?* called the Recognition Register. On their page of the register, each student details his or her ideal work environment, and how to best motivate and reward this person. I find that even for students who can't always articulate their temperament as introverted or extroverted, their preferences can be deduced with high accuracy by studying their responses. The same is likely true for your professional co-workers.

Reframe. There are times when we clash with those around us and instinctively make it a personal affair. Fundamental attribution error drives us to ignore the circumstances that could be affecting the other party's behavior, instead assuming that their flaws or differing opinions are the result of a personal failing. But we know better. We do.

With little exception, disputes such as these escalate because differences of opinion are conflated with differences in work style and worldview. I would challenge you to stop and think as you work, likely internally, to resolve the dispute. Take note of this person's behavior in meetings, writing style, and other factors that could help you frame their actions or reactions in relation to their temperament. You would be surprised at how this context helps you to reframe the individual's actions.

Mind the gap. Laney says about opposite temperaments, "introverts and extroverts line in opposite worlds. Each world has its own language and style of relating. As a result, misunderstandings occur, and gaps of miscommunication develop. However, good communication can close the gaps before they become gulches."

It may sound drastic to say that introverts and extroverts speak different languages. But consider the differing meanings for silence that introverts and extroverts view. To an introvert, silence usually means, "I'm thinking." But that silence to an extrovert can be viewed as a sign of boredom, discomfort, or judgment. Doesn't that seem to you like a misunderstanding that can result from a language barrier?

When gaps of understanding arise, have the humility and courage to approach the situation prepared for "tutoring." Aim to learn what the phrase or action in question really meant. You approaches may vary (extroverts may think nothing of staging such an intervention in real time; introverts may prefer an asynchronous conversation through email or written notes), but the intent should be the same: to seek understanding.

When Personal And Professional Mix

This need for understanding from those around us is needed for professional functions, but can also be especially important when planning events that are a blend of the personal and professional- like workplace parties. Because extroverts gain energy from the very activities that drain it from introverts, the former group can be quick to equate a refusal of an invitation, with a personal judgment. Not so! Well, most of the time. Introverts don't separate themselves from a crowd as a function of judgment, disdain, or boredom. It is equally important to note that refusing an invitation isn't necessarily done out of fear or anxiety, either. More often than not, the battery gauge that reflects their energy level is registering zero and they don't wish to overexert themselves. As we discussed in previous sections, the pleas and guilt trips of friends and colleagues do little to prevent this drain; if anything, they increase the likelihood that the introvert hangover will arrive.

Although the social gatherings that commonly illustrate this principle aren't typically seen in the workplace, there is one time of year where we spend more casual time with colleagues: the holidays. How does your office, department, or division celebrate the holiday season? More often than not, these gatherings are held at the end of a work day, designed to capitalize on a time when staff members are already on campus. They cram many people from different departments on campus together, with designs on allowing people to meet and interact with one another with ease.

There are no ill intentions in all of this, I'm sure. But these sorts of scenarios can be difficult for introverts. And yet, if he or she tries to back out of the party, those silences start to get filled in: "She doesn't want to come to the party? Is she too good to hang out with work people?" "He can't stay? Is he afraid to see us after 5pm?" But again, those assumptions are far more a projection of how the objector feels about the introvert that is seemingly pulling away, than the other way around.

So how do you navigate the dread that can come with the announcement of a work party? Consider some of the following options to make these seasonal gatherings more palatable to your quieter staff members:

Resist the urge to pack multiple departments into one party. Yes, it can be great to see colleagues from other departments at the holiday gathering. But it can also be a rewarding bonding experience to keep holiday gatherings personal by inviting members of your office or department only. One way to determine if the party is getting too big: does this particular group of people meet on a regular basis (once a month or more)? If not, you may be forcing a group together that is simply too large. Use that time to recognize each other for jobs well done over the course of the semester. An intimate affair can be just as much fun as the bigger, more crowded parties can be.

If you must group departments together, allow the party to be a "drop in affair." State in the invitation for these parties that attendees can drop in and out as they please, relieving the burden of the introvert to stay and mingle, lest someone notice that he or she has left. I've worked at an institution where the president did an open house for faculty and staff, but at two different times. That way, the house was not overcrowded all at one time. If I had to guess, I'd say that president was an introvert!

Consider a time or venue change. Another institution I've worked for holds their holiday party in the morning, before the events and minutiae of the day have had time to weigh staff members down. The gathering features brunch (an all-time favorite and much appreciated), a small gift exchange, and time for catching up with one another. It may not seem as though a change in the time of day makes a difference, but it is one way to help introverts avoid the exhaustion that might prevent them from being fully present at the end of a day.

With all of these guidelines for how to best work with introverts, it may be sometimes tempting to wonder if they're worth the effort. I know sometimes I have moments where I can see myself as monumentally difficult to work with! But ultimately, your patience and consideration will be rewarded. Introverts are incredibly attentive by nature, able to pick up otherwise overlooked problems and formulate complex and considerate solutions. They are thoughtful and tactful, able to convey potentially conflict-laden concerns with eloquence. And they are fiercely loyal when comfortable in their work environment. As you look to bring new people to your team, perhaps even from the graduate school pool, see introversion not as an obstacle to overcome or cope with, but as an asset that can be effectively harnessed and learned from.

INsights

⇒ Own the skill and insight that was entrusted to you when you earned the position you're in. Even in moments of doubt, following a mistake, or in the wake of a disappointment, remember: your brain will try to tell you that you don't deserve to be where you are. Not so!

⇒ Draw upon your natural strengths to supplement the work you do each day. If you make an observation that others don't notice, find a method to speak up.

⇒ Inform others about your preferred work style early. Do you need to block off time on your calendar for yourself at the beginning or end of each day? Do you struggle at meetings without an agenda to organize your thoughts?

Let someone know that these things are essential to your success. It's not special treatment; rather, it's articulating the conditions that you need to do your best work.

⇒ If given the opportunity to speak up for the needs of other introverts in the work place (and I promise, it's not just you!), do so. Advocate for scheduling that allows introverts to be at their best, and push for activities to be offered where introverts can thrive more naturally.

⇒ When working with students, make yourself available to hear their needs early on. Provide opportunities for all your student employees or student leaders to let you know, privately, how they work, what they need, and how they like to be recognized. This way, you can be attentive of the conditions in which they work and how you can make them more comfortable.

CHAPTER SEVEN
The Introverted Graduate Student

Graduate school is an interesting and conflicted time for many introverts. On the one hand, the type of learning is nearly ideal- a narrow scope of interest, courses that are clearly interconnected, and assignments that utilize our natural propensity to focus deeply. But the challenge arises when the demanding academics are accompanied by the dichotomous nature of academia. William

Pannapacker illuminates this dichotomy well:

> Many people are drawn to academic life because they expect it will provide a refuge from the social demands of other careers: they believe one can be valued as a studious introvert, as many undergraduates are. But academe is a profession of opposites. Long periods of social isolation- reading and writing- are punctuated by brief periods of intense social engagement: job interviews, teaching, conferences, and meetings [...] and there are few if any supports in place for those students who struggle with the extremes of introversion and extroversion that academe demands.

Interestingly, the world of presenting and defending academic papers combines with networking needs and cocktail hours to present a confusing picture of a domain typically seen to be perfect for introverts. As Cassidy mentioned when she spoke about separation in graduate school, the social demands of the cohort model added an additional level of difficulty to navigating relationships. When your classmates double as your colleagues, each turned-down invitation carries the added weight of affecting professional relationships down the road.

Graduate programs in student affairs or higher education can seem particularly daunting for the sorts of students they tend to attract. I remember realizing fairly early in my graduate journey, that my classroom was populated by students who had all been the first to speak up in their undergraduate classes. For a time, I think I allowed that notion to overcome me, and it affected my willingness to raise my voice in class. But as the cohort grew closer and we learned more about one another, I came to a few conclusions. First, we were all intimidated! We all had moments when we weren't sure if we were supposed to be there. By appealing to each other's areas of interest or expertise, we created an environment where we were (mostly) free to speak our minds. Secondly, and of equal importance, I discovered I wasn't the only introvert in the group. Introverts, being prone to internalization, generally believe they are the only ones feeling or thinking as they are. But by finding other kindred spirits who shared my temperament, I built a level of comfort with my classmates that allow me to count many of them among my closest friends today.

Alliances, both like the one I built with Jeff (mentioned in Chapter Three), as well as ones I created with more introverted colleagues, can be helpful when navigating the sometimes intimidating landscape of a practically-based graduate education. So many opportunities lie before graduate students in this field, and we expect herculean pursuit of all of them. Assistantships, internships, practica, publication, presentations, and professional association boards...I could go on, but you catch my meaning. The options presented are dizzying. And not unlike our perspective on the undergraduate experience, we frown upon those who are not in a tizzy of activity during the duration of their waking hours. So how does an introvert cope with a myriad of demands on time and energy that can't always be relied upon?

Aspire to depth, not breadth. There will be a temptation to overcommit. Fight it. There will be thoughts of inadequacy for not being able to say yes to every opportunity. Banish them. The nature of introversion invites these feelings of doubt because we know more about our perspective than we do anyone else's. But this deep self-awareness can serve as an asset in this instance. What do you really like? What are you really good at? If you are a good presenter, concentrate on making your impact through presentation proposals and opportunities. If you're particularly interested in publishing articles on a topic, seek out opportunities to be featured and concentrate on that venue. Focus your efforts toward opportunities that energize and interest you. Pay special attention to that word, *energize*. That depth will serve you as well as breadth could serve extroverts; you'll be able to effectively harness your natural ability to concentrate meaningfully, and you won't live in fear of forgetting one of so many commitments.

Explore your interests. A related point to the previous one: take the two years of graduate school to find out what you're good at. A research mindset and unprecedented access to written resources (sometimes your access to library materials is greater as a student than as a staff member, so take advantage while you can!) creates a powerful opportunity to learn deeply about any topic in the field you might want to explore more. This research could help you realize what opportunities you want to take on before you leave your program, possibly helping guide future research or employment interests.

Seek out the superconnectors. The prospect of putting yourself out there to meet new people or sell yourself with ones you already know, can feel exhausting before you've even attempted a connection. But don't let the butterflies in your stomach overcome your will to introduce yourself. Don't give in to the butterflies; seek them out. Having an ally in your networking efforts, be it an extrovert or a more comfortable introvert, will help give you a natural entry point into a conversation that introverts occasionally struggle to create. Sophia Dembling calls small talk "the WD-40 of society." She goes on to credit it for "keep[ing] the gears of society cranking smoothly, mak[ing] the world feel friendly and protect[ing] our social muscles from atrophy." Don't let discomfort or potential exhaustion rust your gears, keep them moving with the help of a friend!

Find your refuge. Even if you love the people you're taking class with, even if you have wonderful and understanding roommates, even if you pace yourself and don't get overwhelmed often...now and again, you're going to need a break. Take the time needed to find your own personal "fortress of solitude", somewhere that you can sleep, study, or recharge undisturbed. I have a thing about parks, and do my best to find one near my house to unwind. I have been known to pull on my running shoes for a free hour to myself during retreats. I also get a great deal from heading to the beach with a good book and a pair of earplugs. Your refuge could look like any of these things, or it could be something completely different. But the essential element of this refuge is its ability to effectively recharge you. Like I discussed earlier in the book, it must have a real outlet, allow for adequate time to recharge, and be as free of "power shortages" as possible.

Monitor yourself and stand up for your needs. Recognizing your need for a break or recharge and being able to remove yourself from a situation to act on it are two very different things. I can't tell you how many times I've set a time to leave a networking event or outing with friends, only to find myself ignoring my need to rest for the sake of preserving social graces. This is a tempting notion for those who are accustomed to not disrupting the atmosphere of an event. That being said, it's okay to stand up for yourself and honor your needs. Adam McHugh puts it beautifully when he says,

> No is an indispensable word for introverts who need solitude and space to refuel and reflect. Without 'no', we are unable to fully engage with others and to engage with others and to exercise our gifts in our communities. Saying 'no' at times enables us to wholeheartedly say 'yes' at other times.

Whenever I find myself struggling with the decision to stay or go, I recall some of the reactions I've had to reaching that burnout point in public. It rarely goes well, and can sometimes lead to rude or snippy exchanges that I know I'll regret. Combat the possibility of an adverse reaction by listening to the inner voice that says "Time to go!" It knows best, I promise.

Building these habits early in your career in this field will go a long way to helping you establish healthy and temperamentally appropriate habits to preserve your sanity and energy in this often demanding profession.

At the same time, a better understanding and ability to manage your introverted tendencies isn't always enough to improve your station in life. For that reason, I will provide tips on how supervisors and institutions can help level the proverbial playing field for those who can otherwise be overly stimulated by standard operating procedure. I offer as an example Julia, whose graduate assistantship fair experience cemented her suspicions of her own introversion. When asked about a situation that helped her realize her introversion, she mentioned "the Open House in the C[ollege] S[tudent] A[ffairs] program where I walked up those stairs and the MSC (Marshall Student Center) and seriously considered turning right around."

Can we, as college administrators and instructors, remove all the obstacles and challenges to temperament? No, nor am I of the belief that we should try. But in areas where it may (a) push away otherwise qualified talent, or (b) obscure our overall objective, some measures can be taken to ensure success regardless of temperament. So how can "institutional temperamentism" be reduced in graduate programs?

Consider a change in assistantship interview format. For many prospective graduate students, the assistantship interview is one of their first significant exposures to the program. Should that early contact be daunting, alienating, and exhausting? Or is there another way to complete this task? Interviews conducted en masse in a cavernous hall is great preparation for placement conferences and other like interviewing scenarios, but it's also quite impersonal as an introduction to a program that hopefully emphasizes personal connection and individual attention.

What sorts of alternatives can you brainstorm that could take advantage of the introvert's natural tendencies? Consider changes as small as allowing interviews to take place at an offbeat location (such as an on campus coffee shop or adjacent conference room), or as innovative as taking the candidate to your office and having him or her perform a job-related task. This reimagining of a standard process could yield more comfort for the interviewee and, as a result, a better view of what your candidate is capable of.

Discuss expectations of graduate work, and the differences between it and undergraduate academics. The heightened focus and intensity of a graduate program is typically evident through a brief perusal of a course catalog or a discussion with professors. However, the culture shift that networking and presentations of research create is not always as evident. Make sure to illuminate this element of graduate work in information sessions and orientation programs that surround entry to a graduate program.

Again, these are not scenarios that introverts are incapable of functioning in; with adequate preparation and an understanding of what lies ahead, these are situations in which an introvert can actually excel. But their fortune favors preparation, and a realistic view of the years ahead can help to foster comfort with this change in academic expectations.

Vary presentation formats. I don't make this recommendation to allow introverted students to hide from public speaking, but rather to afford them an opportunity to present their ideas in a venue that takes advantage of their deep thoughts and deliberative nature. Could a presentation be given in the form of an artistic piece, pre-recorded video, or even dance performance? While it may seem unorthodox, it could be interesting to see how the introvert's natural propensity to connect ideas manifests itself "outside the lines".

Install or maintain a student mentorship program. Because introverts thrive in relationships requiring depth, a student mentorship element to a graduate program can allow them to ease into the rigor of a graduate program under the watchful eye of an older student who can address their questions and concerns. Particularly for students who are initially maladjusted, a close relationship where these concerns can be shared with impunity, a pairing with a more experienced student can be helpful. Activities for these pairs need not be mandated; students can determine how deep or shallow these relationships go. The important thing is to connect an incoming student with someone to show him or her the proverbial ropes early on, to prevent feelings of alienation or incompetence that could derail academic success.

For many aspiring student affairs professionals,

graduate school is the first opportunity to see what our field is about, and where they will fit in the landscape of the profession. If we truly wish to show them that success is possible in this field regardless of temperament, it must start here. Introverts in theory-heavy programs will thrive, as their brains work to focus deeply on learning the content presented. Practically focused programs could engage the introvert equally well, allowing him or her to focus on applying class lessons to the office and interactions with students. In either case, this concentrated introduction to the field is a crucial point for students trying to find their place in the field.

INsights

⇒ Establish a working routine early on, and protect it fiercely. Need your full Saturday morning to do your reading? Perhaps you can't do late-night study sessions because the rest of the day wears you out? Let your classmates know how you work. They'll make time to understand you.

⇒ Say no when needed! Yes, grad school is a

time to take advantage of lots of opportunities, but the consequences of pushing your limits are physiologically stronger for introverts. If you truly feel strained or overwhelmed, ask for help or graciously and responsibility step away from a task that could push you over the edge.

⇒ With that said, challenge yourself. A push out of your comfort zone now and again is needed in this work, so try new things if you can!

⇒ For those working with graduate students, check in with them often to ensure that their workload and professional exploration are going well. Provide opportunities to reflect, in a variety of forms. This time is crucial for carving out a professional path; help students aspire to balance cultivation of a professional identity, with the demands of schoolwork that will provide their foundation for professional competency.

CHAPTER EIGHT
The Introverted Conferencegoer

Conference season is an unavoidable period of tightly controlled chaos in our profession. As we weave our schedules together to represent ourselves and our institutions at regional and annual meetings for a host of acronym-named organizations, all while continuing to be effective in our daily roles, we can become overwhelmed and overstimulated. However, despite the occasional difficulties we face while navigating these frenetic time periods, we appreciate the rewarding opportunities they provide to delve deeper into areas of interest. Further, they allow us to connect with people we may not have met in person or seen for some time. So although the introvert's conference experience may be a more taxing one than that of the extrovert, it isn't an insurmountable challenge to take on.

In this section, I want to concentrate on elements of the conference experience that haven't yet been discussed. So rather than addressing the networking and presenting piece of the conference experience, I'd like to talk more about the selection of conferences, narrowing of session attendance, and mitigating the effects of a hyper-stimulating environment.

Before the Conference
Scheduling
Each year, we map out our conference schedules and select what experiences we'd like to partake in, based on a variety of factors. Some of us choose conferences based on our own professional affiliations or the functional areas we work in on a daily basis. And truthfully, some of us don't get to dictate our conference delegacy, instead

representing our institutions at the behest of a director or other institutional official. But for those with a little more flexibility, consider choosing conferences that are well suited to your temperament.

Do you live in a city that may be hosting a conference? If you can find benefit in it, consider attending: travel costs will stay low; your chances of unanticipated overstimulation will be reduced in a familiar environment; and you'll get to sleep in your own bed each night, a tremendous benefit when doing your required recharging.

Another option that could reduce the chances of "catastrophic overstimulation" could be attending a regional conference or institute, rather than a national conference or annual meeting. These conferences tend to be smaller, allowing for easier movement. They cater to issues in a specific region or topic area, narrowing their focus from the "fire hose" feeling that we may get from some larger conferences. And if you attend a regional conference in your own region, proximity will heighten the chances of seeing and interacting with people you already know. Similarly, attending an institute on a specific topic is likely to gather people of a like mind, allowing you to converse with people you could be at ease with.

Finally, consider drive-in conferences as a means to get short bursts of professional development and networking experience, all while minimizing your time away from the office. These day to two-day long experiences have the comfort and proximity benefits of a regional conference, but also allow for built in processing time in the form of a commute. I know that after some drive-in conferences, I've felt fully recharged by the time I arrived home, just because of the extra hour to two hours I had in the car to digest what I'd learned. Sometimes a walk to a hotel room isn't enough to allow the day's musings to sink in; the added time in relative isolation could do wonders for your retention of information as well as your sanity.

For those of you who attend conferences with students, work with them as they try to map their schedules for the semester. Some will be concerned about classwork, exams, and other on-campus commitments that they will be missing while they are gone. Work with them to assuage these fears, encouraging them to reach out to professors and make arrangements regarding missed work, and to delegate responsibilities to other organization members in their absence.

Accommodations

At a time where institutions are, to turn a phrase from the theme of *Good Times*, "scratchin' and survivin'", accommodations can be a tricky element of the conference experience to maneuver. Typically, institutions will request that multiple professional delegates share a room for the duration of the conference experience. In their minds, the cost is lower and staff members will have an opportunity to bond. No problem!

But the introverts on many staffs have a difficult time with this forced togetherness. Not because they don't like the people they're with, necessarily, but because roommates (especially ones that we don't get to choose, which can happen) may not always understand the unique needs of an introvert when it comes to processing. It is also worth noting that, for those who fall close to the line of the introvert/extrovert scale on Myers-Briggs, the question "do you consider yourself to be territorial?" is an often-used one to break the proverbial tie. Those who answer yes are more likely to be territorial. And as my favorite President Abraham Lincoln famously noted, "A house divided itself cannot stand." And a hotel room divided gets pretty cramped, pretty quickly.

So how do we navigate this occasional inevitability of the conference experience? First, discuss with your supervisor the benefits of staying alone, or with a roommate of your choosing. Whether your chosen ally is introverted or extroverted, it should be someone who understands your need for decompression time, *not just someone you're friends with*. Just as we've realized when pairing roommates in housing scenarios, your roommate doesn't have to be your best friend; he or she just needs to be someone you can live with in relative peace. With professionals, and where conferences are concerned, the same rules apply. If you state your case convincingly, including how you'll likely be better equipped to bring back useful information when given time and space to digest it fully, your proposal may gain more traction.

If your request is denied, and you must share space,

get creative! Carve out time in your day that is just for you. It may require getting up an hour earlier to head to the gym or take a walk around the host city, or it may mean you stay up a little later to watch TV in a hotel lounge or read in the hallway. However you best decompress, make sure to build that time into your schedule, especially if you're concerned you may not have that time otherwise. Don't neglect your needs as an introvert, for the effects could be disastrous.

Similarly, should you have students who you sense are introverted and will have a difficult time sharing space, speak with the whole group about taking time to decompress during the conference. Those who need the time away will feel validated in that need and likely act on the advice; those who don't may take it anyway, and find value in the quiet and solitude!

Session Selection
The long brain pathway characteristic of the introverted mind makes quick decisions more difficult. This can be true when selecting the color of a shirt to buy, picking wrapping paper for a gift, or—my personal least favorite decision—picking a

restaurant for lunch or dinner. This difficulty in making quick decisions understandably extends into our work, and can affect the ability to select conference sessions to attend. Particularly at bigger conferences, where the options are seemingly endless, deciding where we want to be can be extremely challenging.

A great friend of the introvert is time; be sure to give yourself some. Conference schedules can appear weeks in advance of the actual meeting. Use that extra time to your advantage, perusing the offerings and marking those that you're interested in. Even if there isn't a time assigned to the sessions yet, this strategy can ensure that you have the time to decide in a leisurely fashion what you'd like to learn about. Be sure to make more selections than there are time slots. This way, if there are cancellations or changes to the program, you have a backup plan. Shifting gears in the absence of a backup plan can be difficult for introverts, so being prepared for the possibility is always a good idea.

Team up with colleagues or student delegates from your and other institutions if you find that you want to see more than one session in a given time block. Taking copious notes during sessions can keep you attentive and focused, but could also pay dividends to other delegates from your institution interested in a similar topic. Dividing and conquering conference blocks is a great way to learn from other delegates while stretching the precious dollars that sent you to the meeting in the first place.

During the Conference
Map Out the Day Early
Have an idea of where you'd like to be at various points during the day. When selecting sessions of interest, make sure to also take note of where they are, and how long it will take to get from one place to another. Conference scheduling "apps" are available with increasing frequency; downloading the app for your conference may automate much of this process for you. When a pathway is set, both in your mind and in your conference booklet (or electronic schedule), the overstimulation and anxiety that can come with real-time navigation is lessened considerably, freeing your mind to learn attentively from the presenters in the room. To that end, be attentive to any room or topic changes that may have occurred for the day. Being able to

anticipate these changes will also lessen potential stress. And one final way to lessen your potential for overprogramming- schedule free time in your day! Laurie Helgoe remarks in *Introvert Power*, "planned time becomes a demand, which, paradoxically, is not time at all." Ensure that there are moments in each day for which there are no demands on your time. Your brain, heart, and soul will thank you!

Capture Your Learning
Whether you choose to take notes, create recordings (with the permission of the presenter, of course!), or even create doodles, capturing the information that you gather at conferences is essential. Many introverts digest information better through writing, and being diligent about this process can help you retain more content at a time when your brain may otherwise be in overdrive. As I mentioned previously, these notes can help other conference delegates gain insight into sessions they could not attend, and also help jog your memory when sharing learned information after your return to the office.

Don't be afraid to share your learning in real time!

Permission to live Tweet or share interesting tidbits over Facebook is becoming increasingly common and permissible during conference sessions. A 2012 study from Michigan State University revealed that students in the classroom are more engaged with, and better retain content, that they are permitted to Tweet. Why should that phenomenon be any different for professionals in a conference scenario? Although the practice is becoming more common, it is not yet universally permissible; when in doubt, ask your presenter or notify him or her beforehand if you're concerned about appearing inattentive.

If you are attending a conference with students, discuss with them how they will capture the content that they learn, with an eye on sharing it with others when they return to campus. Perhaps your campus requires nightly time to share tidbits of what was learned, and reflection on how it could be implemented on campus. Practices such as this can help students put into perspective what they're learning, and help them focus amidst the high volume of information being shared.

Maintain and Rekindle Connections
An advantage that conferences have over other

long-distance forms of professional development is their ability to gather people. Colleagues from around the country and world converge on a single space, energized about their work and interested in meeting others who share their excitement. Capitalize on this energy and allow it to energize you, but in small amounts. Rather than attempting to plug in your proverbial charger at crowded conference socials, instead carve out time to meet with old friends or connections made online. Cassidy S. plans a few coffee dates ahead of the conference with friends, mentors, or online connections in advance, holding herself to those appointments as though they were meetings back on her home campus. The promise of energy-granting conversation and understanding are too precious and tantalizing to give up, so make sure to include a few of these in your conference-going experience.

Should you decide to tackle the conference socials, make sure to take any cues your body gives you during the experience. If you sense your energy dipping, find a way to recharge in the room (volunteering to take pictures or complete a task for a committee member are two ways that Marti Laney recommends recharging without leaving), or step out briefly to collect and reorient yourself. And when it's time to go, it's time to go. Be gracious in your departure, but then retreat to a place of solitude to restore equilibrium.

Don't Skip Meals
This may seem like a minor point, but it is an important one. I was shocked, but also partially vindicated, to learn from Marti Laney's research that introverts are not only in need of more constant caloric intake than their extroverted counterparts, but they are more sensitive to the lows that come from delaying or skipping food. Remember the operative phrase "easily overstimulated"? As it happens, hunger and the distraction it can provide is a stimulating force that can draw energy from introverts. Because the mind moves so constantly with introverts, fuel for all that thinking (not to mention your other essential bodily functions) is at a premium. This is of particular relevance at conferences; since they can be an uncomfortable or unnatural state for introverts, it is in their best interest to stay fueled, so make sure to pack extra snacks and plan for consistent mealtimes to avoid any taxing energy lows.

After the Conference

Gather and Purge

I always come home from conferences with far more "stuff" than I left with. Business cards, pamphlets, session handouts, and other paraphernalia from the experience pile up over the course of a few days, and it can be overwhelming to sift through. But commit yourself to focusing your takeaways by consolidating your materials. As you pore over the items you've received, consider what information you can truly take back to your coworkers, what initiatives or vendors you plan to implement on your own campus, or even what materials could be cited in your own research or other work. If it doesn't fit one of these three needs, it can more than likely be thrown away, recycled, or given away. The act of consolidating your conference materials is a physical act designed to restore much needed normalcy in the aftermath of a frenzied conference experience. Don't hesitate to take that time to "come back down" after your return.

Summarize

The closely related cousin of gathering and purging

is summarizing. Again, the fire-hose-strength spray of information you're presented with at a conference can overwhelm anyone who doesn't stop after the experience is done to distill it. Take time after you leave the conference, but before you return to the office, to take stock of what you learned, what you want to share with colleagues, what ideas you hope to implement, and other key takeaways from your experience. Taking this moment to remember the significant moments and lessons from your conference experience will help you to recall them, and will help them stand out in your mind as you return to a normal routine. The energy that you expend on the excitement of your experience is precious- don't let it go to waste by letting it get buried under day-to-day obligations and the status quo in your office!

Follow Up with New Friends
You may have come away from the conference with many new acquaintances to contact, or presenters that you have further questions for. Don't let the desire to strengthen those connections disappear as you return to your everyday routine! Connections are hard to make for introverts, so when they present themselves, it is important to honor and

pursue them. These connections could yield the energizing deep conversations that so many introverts crave, and will allow you to take the perspective of someone in a new environment. Keep these relationships going after your shared time together ends; you never know how these ties could grow!

Again, if you're attending with student delegates, encourage them to network with their fellow students. While it may not lead to the same sorts of opportunities that our networking provides, they could learn more from the students they meet, get new perspectives on the initiatives taking place on other campuses, and utilize their opinions as a way to gauge success of their own ideas.

Alternatives to Conferences
For some professionals, conferences aren't going to be an option. Whether the obstacle is external (lack of funding or institutional support) or internal (apprehension, discomfort with or fear of travel or attendance), these experiences may simply be out of your reach. There are still many ways that introverts can connect meaningfully with these powerful professional development experiences. Below are a

few, and of course there are many others. If you have questions about how to get involved, look to friends or colleagues who may be involved with professional organizations. They're sure to know of a way for you to get involved!

Conference Proposal Review
As I have mentioned a few times previously, many introverts consider themselves to be readers. Conference proposal review is a great way for introverts to harness this strength while also examining the content upon which conference presentations are built. Individuals with a deep interest in the topic being addressed will love the ability to explore multiple institutions' approaches to our work that proposal review affords. And if you're interested in more information about a proposal that you read, you can always contact the presenter (after the chosen programs are announced, of course) for more information about their work. It provides a low-stakes, but highly informative, method by which introverts can learn about topics in which they might be interested.

Webinars, Chats, and Structured Conversations
Our learning as professionals is no longer bound to

our ability to be physically present in a location. Virtual conference opportunities to attend NASPA and ACPA are proving that this learning can be shared virtually, and can provide a very real alternative to the hustle and bustle of the energy-intensive "face to face" option. Webinars, online chats, and structured conversations allow you to listen to colleagues and experts across the country, from relative comfort behind your computer screen. You can listen and digest information at roughly your own pace, chiming in with questions either through a call-in or through an electronic message. If you do miss something or want to refer to notes for any reason, these electronic learning sessions are typically followed with links to recordings and additional resources in a more expedient manner than some in-person conference experiences. And should you feel simultaneously bold and shy, these virtual presenting forums are a way to share your own expertise without the daunting imagery of a crowd staring at you, hanging on your every word. Although the value of this sort of professional engagement is often questioned, they continue to get better and more engaging, and hold promise for those wishing to learn from home or the office.

"Unconferences" and "Confabs"

In recent years, a less formal, more collaborative form of conference known as the unconference has joined the formal proposal, acceptance, and presentation process for professional conferences. The unconference, and its close relative the *confab*, are designed to be informal conversations about topics of interest. The subjects of these conversations, which can be conducted either in-person or online via social media, are selected by those participating in the conversation. They may be moderated, but ultimately are designed to allow all in attendance to contribute to a conversation. Unconferences and confabs can be tremendous equalizers, allowing participants of all ages and levels of experience to speak their mind about the topic at hand. When effectively moderated, they can be a powerful way to gather opinions about issues in the field, and can also yield a multitude of solutions to issues that plague us all.

The student affairs conference can be at once a highly valuable and positively exhausting experience for the introverted conferencegoer. With preparation, an understanding of what you'll be experiencing, and a healthy level of respect for your own boundaries, you can thrive in a seemingly hostile environment, learning a great deal and making new personal connections along the way.

INsights

⇒ Do what you can to prepare for the conference in advance. Pack snacks! Book travel early to allow for reduced stress travel! Plan what sessions you'll be attending using schedules released prior to your arrival.

⇒ If you opt to stay with people, recognize that you may need time *away* from those who you're sharing space with. Plan to walk around the host city, work out early, or escape to a coffee shop for some solitary recharge time. Your brain will thank you!

⇒ Make connections in advance. Via social media or around the office, try to determine who will be there in advance to reduce any anxiety of "going in cold."

⇒ If conferences truly aren't your cup of tea, don't fret! There are a number of ways to get involved with the knowledge shared at these gatherings from afar, or to attend smaller versions of these "meetings of the minds."

CHAPTER NINE
The Introverted Educator

My greatest act of rebellion in high school had little to do with skipping school or disregarding the dress code (though let's be honest, both happened). No, the most significant act of disobedience I displayed during my time at C. Leon King High School was changing my own schedule.

My fourth period Higher Level Biology Class was,

to put it nicely, madness. How our administrators managed to match a group of students so simultaneously brilliant, and absolutely *done* with the organized learning process, is beyond me. Classes were loud, unfocused, and hard to follow for students who needed quiet and time to process and discuss material. When I voiced my frustrations to friends taking the same class during first period, they seemed puzzled. Their classroom environment didn't seem to resemble the one I was describing. During a first period study hall, I decided to check it out, going to their class to take notes I hadn't been able to get during a previous class period. The change in my efficacy during that class was shocking.

Armed with my knowledge of the drastically different class environments, I went to our guidance counselor to request a schedule change. I told her about my struggles to learn in my class, and how much easier it was for me to concentrate and contribute in the other class. But despite making (what I believed to be) a good case, my request was denied.

So I created what we'd now call a "life hack": I used

my first period study hall to go to biology. I asked that teacher for a pass to that class, sat in, took all my notes, and even participated in lab assignments with that class, and returned to study hall at the end of the period. When I returned fourth period, my teacher permitted me to get a pass to a study hall, knowing full well that I didn't need to sit in on the class a second time. After a few weeks of this, our guidance office relented and let me switch classes.

I'll admit, this incident happened right at that point in high school where all the students itched to rebel. But I'd also like to grant that my behavior was exceptional in comparison to my fellow students. Many who find themselves in learning environments that are a poor fit, won't speak up about it. Even fewer will take action. But I'd like to keep this scenario in mind as we discuss the role of the educator in crafting a good learning environment for introverts.

The overwhelming majority of student affairs professionals are in a position to teach the students they work with. Whether you are permitted to do so from the front of a lecture hall or classroom, or instead do so in alternate venues like offices, dining halls, challenge courses, or even student leader interviews, few of us are devoid the opportunity to impart knowledge on the students we encounter each day.

We have long understood that for one reason or another, a "one size fits all" approach to student learning actually fits very few. Many of these differences have been attributed to learning styles; increasing research dictates that temperament also plays a significant role in how we take in, store, and process information. Consider this description of the average classroom of our time, as described by Marti Laney in *The Hidden Gifts of the Introverted Child*:

> Typical classrooms consume gallons of fuel because they are noisy, full of visual distractions, and require close proximity to others. It's difficult to hear, especially if people speak quickly or have accents. And on top of all this, there's often little time or space to recharge.

Schmeck and Lockhart (1983) elaborate on this dichotomy and how the brain responds to it:

> [...] because it takes very little stimulation for introverts to perceive a stimulus, their brains become easily overstimulated. Thus they tend to seek out an environment where there is relatively little stimulation. Extroverts, on the other hand, require strong stimulation to perceive a stimulus and tend to seek out environments that provide relatively large amounts of stimulation.

While these descriptions were written about K-12 classrooms and the stimulation levels within them, little changes by the time these students, beleaguered by exhausting primary and secondary school learning environments, arrive in our hallowed halls. Knowing that the typical classroom appears more like the high stimulation environment that Schmeck and Lockhart describe as ideal for extroverts, it is no wonder that we encounter students so seemingly frustrated with the concept of higher learning- if years of learning fought your natural proclivity to learn, wouldn't you be frustrated too?

As educators, we tend to see students who seem

inattentive or disconnected from classroom content as it is typically presented as apathetic, uninterested, or troublesome. Interestingly enough, introverted educators occasionally share this perception of introverted learners! A study published in 2011 discovered that teachers from across the K-12 spectrum rated, in a hypothetical classroom, quiet students as the least intelligent when compared to students who were talkative or otherwise "typical" in their behavior. So it would appear that something in the teacher education process could be encouraging educators to favor our more vocal learners. So where does this leave their quieter counterparts, particularly once they arrive in college hoping to have a more fulfilling experience?

First things first, we as educators, regardless of temperament, must redefine our ingrained notions of what a successful student looks like. To equate garrulousness and ease of speaking with competency and success does a disservice to their more contemplative counterparts. Susan Cain often says, "There is zero correlation between being the best talker, and having the best ideas." But it's easy to forget this in a room full of students, faced with silence, and a strong voice speaks up to break the tense quiet. We tend to revere that person for being "brave enough" to start us off, not realizing that the bravery looks far different for those who process slower and speak more selectively. In fact, in the scenario that started this chapter, the brave part for me was collecting my thoughts in a fashion eloquent enough to approach an administrator with hopes of making a change. Even as an introvert, I catch myself favoring those students when selecting student leaders for panels, interviews, or other opportunities to highlight examples of involvement. But this is a habit that, with practice, we can break.

I wrote an article for *Campus Activities Programming Magazine* in 2012 about how to work with introverted students in some of the more common educational capacities we encounter, namely student leader selection and training. Below you'll find an excerpt of that article with a few strategies on how to incorporate introverted students into groups in a manner that suits their nature. I find that while these reminders can be helpful for extroverts who may not think about how select practices affect introverted students, it can be equally important to jog the memory of introverts who may not remember the effect such practices had on their own development.

Plan downtime in your schedule- both in training and in yearlong programming schedules. With an orientation toward the inner world, introverts are drained of energy fairly quickly when constantly interacting with the outside world. During training sessions or retreats, periodic breaks will allow those who need the time to internalize and process information to be more effective when they return to the large group. The same should also be true for your yearly programming schedule. Without adequate time between events, we as educators run the risk of creating a system that doesn't allow students to learn from the work that they do. Emphasizing fewer quality events over a greater number of events allows not just more substantial events, but students will ultimately have a greater chance to learn from the events that they're presenting.

Weigh group, individual, and written portions of applications equally. A strength of introverts is the ability to express themselves very well in writing. Additionally, those who can express themselves verbally may prefer to do so more slowly, taking time to think about responses. We mustn't mistake this inconsistency between action and written word as disingenuous, nor should we assume those who are slow to answer are unprepared. In building your programming board, be prepared to assess the value of your candidates across multiple media and in many different scenarios. Just because someone wilts in a circle of candidates doesn't mean he doesn't have anything to say, or that she isn't willing to work in a group. Allow candidates to express themselves in a manner that they are most comfortable with, and you may end up with a few potential leaders that you wouldn't have had otherwise!

Allow for multiple forms of expression in reflection processes. Even once an introvert is a member of a board, they may be cautious when speaking up in a group, or even in a one-on-one meeting with an advisor. Ensure that the introverts of the group have a chance to say what they need to say in a manner that is most comfortable for them. Have a student who doesn't speak up in one-on-ones? Give him or her the option of journaling each week, or encourage emailing of ideas after meetings when everyone has had time to process the content shared. By helping students become comfortable expressing their thoughts, they will be come empowered to do even better work in an organization that understands their needs.

Help students understand how each other work. Even as the introverts begin to understand themselves, they still run the risk of being misunderstood by their extroverted coworkers. Including a session in your retreat or training on group dynamics can combat this. Present the Myers-Briggs Type Indicator or Big 5 Personality Theory to your students, showing them the difference between the two concepts. Detail the differences in work style, temperament, and strengths of each style, and emphasize that these seemingly dualistic states are actually opposite points of a continuum. Everyone has aspects of introversion and extroversion- these qualities should not be used to polarize, but rather to help foster understanding in the group.

You may be asking, "what if I don't work on a scale that allows for use of these larger ideas?" Sometimes you don't have an opportunity to weigh multiple forms of expression or building in processing time if you're an academic advisor who meets with students in short increments, or a financial aid advisor that may only see students in response to specific questions. To that, I would say that there are other tips that you can employ to ensure comfort for introverted students during your interactions. Below are a few that I put together for our orientation team in preparation for interviews with leader candidates, adapted to fit many types of encounters we may have with students:

Temper the atmosphere of the room to create comfort. In baking, to "temper" a substance such as eggs or chocolate is to bring down the temperature gradually to prevent it from breaking or cooking too quickly. Sometimes students, particularly those who are new to a structured one-on-one advising or meeting process, need us to temper the interview situation to allow them to be the best versions of themselves. This includes introducing yourself warmly, welcoming them to the room, and letting them know that the encounter is a conversation, nothing more. With that said, this should not be an invitation to not take the meeting seriously. We need to know that these students are capable of being professional, and these encounters are the first place we'll likely get to see that competency from them. Strive to create an unintimidating, but professional, environment.

Patiently allow time for the student to respond. Even for the most prepared students, a response to a direct question doesn't always come quickly. Let the student know at the outset that it's okay to take a moment to think about a question before responding, and hold true to that promise. Make sure that your nonverbal cues match this voiced patience- if they feel you are getting impatient, it could affect their performance.

This timing piece is critical for introverted students, and as such has been mentioned many times in this book. You would be surprised at how an extra few minutes with an introvert can bring forth a wealth of knowledge that may not have moved to the forefront as quickly as it would for an extrovert.

To return to extroverts for a moment, what about them? Much of this chapter has spoken about how introverted educators can work with introverted students. But, as we know, they are not the only students we work with. Introverted students will also need to be able to effectively interact with, create learning environments for, and summon the success of, extroverted students. And just as introverted students suffer when forced to adopt the learning practices of extroverts, so too will the extroverts underperform in an environment that doesn't allow them to flourish naturally. Schmeck and Lockhart illustrate the struggle to balance educating across the temperamental spectrum as they note:

If you find yourself wanting to say that either the introverted or extroverted pattern is "right" or "better," your own behavior probably fits that pattern. As is true of most personality characteristics, it is easiest for introverts to appreciate the style of other introverts and for extroverts to appreciate the style of other extroverts [...] most students are neither totally introverted nor totally extroverted. They require both a quiet and stimulating learning environments.

But just as students aren't able to opt out of certain obligations based on temperament, introverted educators cannot design classrooms that allow those with different dominant temperaments to fail. So what can we do to be considerate of our extroverted students, without ignoring the need for students challenged by the norm?

Create multiple methods for students to contribute. This recommendation is a different configuration of the earlier advice offered about weighing group input, written assignments, and one-on-one encounters equally. If the topic you're covering allows for it, consider letting students select the method of delivery for their assignments. Those who are more inclined to best express themselves in writing can do so, while those who thrive in groups can opt to take that route. All methods are valuable, and it will not always be feasible for students to select the most appropriate option, but occasionally offering the option could allow talents to shine that could otherwise remain hidden.

Educate more energetic students on the benefits of contemplative quiet time. Just because the ability to sit quietly and enjoy contemplative time comes naturally to introverts, doesn't mean that extroverted students can't benefit from the ability to cultivate contemplative tendencies. Consider incorporating time for reflection into daily or weekly lessons, with time to journal, draw, or even stretch or practice yoga into your educational offerings. In an increasingly fast-paced world, even the most gregarious of our students will value the time to "unplug" and hear their own thoughts. It will take some work for many of them, but they will likely appreciate the opportunity.

Be proactive about introducing students to supplemental opportunities to use their strengths. If your classroom or learning space, by its very nature, does lean more toward one temperament than another, seek out opportunities for those who are challenged by that format to shine. For example, if you see community theater opportunities or public speaking opportunities for your more extroverted students, draw their attention to these opportunities and urge them to participate. Not only will they appreciate the chance to use their natural tendencies, they will likely also appreciate your attention to their strengths and the relationship associated with that observation.

INsights

⇒ Consider incorporating "introvert-friendly" strategies into your classroom or learning environment. Defining "participation" by more than just raising your hand can make a world of difference for introverts.

⇒ If you are teaching, recognize that some of these strategies will be difficult for extroverted students- don't teach to one at the expense of the other. While few strategies I recommend don't also help extroverts, understand that some may need more stimulation and attempt to adapt accordingly.

CHAPTER TEN
The Introverted Manager

Conventional wisdom is starting to warm to the idea that the best leader in any given room isn't always the loudest, most charismatic individual who is always first to respond. In fact, recent research by Adam Grant, Francesca Gino, and David Hoffman has actually found that sometimes, introverted leadership is preferable to the more garrulous and showy brand we've become accustomed to in our society. The good news is, those of us who have long been told that we're not cut out for leadership now have a chance to shine. The not-so-good news? With so much leadership training flying in the face of our typical way of being, we can sometimes be at a loss as to how to lead authentically.

Creating Temperament-Friendly Workplaces

As I just mentioned, recent research has shown that some groups are more productive and successful under introverted leadership than under that of the typical extrovert. More specifically, groups of proactive employees were less successful under an extroverted boss. Moreover, college students deemed "proactive" by this study were 28% more successful "under" introverted leadership than they were under extroverted leadership. Why? According to the study,

> More apt to be receptive to the employees' efforts to voice their ideas, the study discovered that 'less extraverted leaders can develop more efficient and effective practices that enhance group effectiveness. That is to

say that more innovations and creative idea sharing can be produced when leaders are willing to listen to others rather than simply doing all the talking themselves. In an economy where creative thinking and innovation are increasingly important to survival and success for businesses, having a leader who cultivates these can be vital.

This article admittedly makes a leap, implying that the more extroverted members of our society struggle with the ability to listen. I'm willing to grant that this is not always true, but we've all encountered the leaders that follow in the footsteps of Jack Welch, who would famously enter rooms of employees proclaiming, "Here's what we should do." Grant, Gino, and Hoffman claim that for groups that are composed of proactive, creative and competent people, the Welch model is far from ideal for encouraging their success. It may follow, then, that the most important skill that an introverted manager can possess is to cultivate a spirit of proactivity in his or her staff.

Build trust and mutual respect. One of the best forms of engagement I've been a part of as a staff member came in graduate school, when my supervisor in my second year instituted trivia contests as part of our staff meetings. Ten questions (and sometimes a bonus) were posed at these meetings each week, and competition became fierce. Rather than being forced to raise hands and speak quickly, responses were written down and checked by each individual. Because the topics on which the questions were based varied wildly, we were able to learn more about each person's outside interests based on the answers they got correct, and it resulted in a fun-loving atmosphere amongst professionals and paraprofessionals who could have fun with one another. We trusted each other and respected one another because we had a means to get to know each other.

For introverts, ease and comfort with sharing ideas and working together is bred from those moments of familiarity; outstanding managers will be able to create opportunities for these moments to arise organically. One of the simplest ways to do this? Listen. Grant, Gino and Hoffman note in their work that "since less extroverted leaders may be more willing to listen to divergent opinions and perspectives, they may be more capable of using [...]

ideas constructively, reinforcing for employees that their ideas are valued."

Permit multiple forms of contribution. Some may need to speak their contributions; others may prefer to write them down. Allow for both, and be vocal about these options. My VPSA knows that I will likely email her after our meetings with thoughts about questions she poses, even forwarding an article that I've drawn a connection to. She teases me for it, but also understands that's how I work. To the first point: cultivate an environment where people *can* understand that's how people work. Some introverted staff members may need to ponder information presented and get back to you later, and some may be more at ease writing about it, sending an email, and in some cases, an expression even more artistic! Sometimes, employees, introverted and extroverted alike, may bring ideas that range from creative to "off the wall". Be receptive to the possibilities that may come from those ideas. Introverted leaders have been proven to be uniquely receptive to these sorts of ideas:

Employees proactive behaviors can introduce

a novel perspective, which may "stimulate divergent attention and thought. As a result, even when they are wrong they contribute to the detection of novel solutions and decisions that, on balance, are qualitatively better."

The introvert's ability to incorporate different types of ideas, feedback, and personalities into productive work and creative solutions is an asset to the introverts aching to contribute in a manner other than just their words, and an asset to the students that could benefit from these unconventional initiatives.

Take control, carefully. Grant, Gino, and Hoffman's study said more about the circumstances under which introverted managers succeed, attributing their high performance to "[being] receptive to employee proactivity as a valuable source of input, communicating in ways that signal openness and interest." As you manage, regardless of your own temperament, be sure to cultivate an environment that is attentive to the potential contributions of introverts, while also providing opportunities for the extroverts to contribute. If you are an introvert, the potential to be overpowered by extroverts exists; find ways to assert yourself and other introverts, making sure that they can be heard without overpowering the environment overall. Karen Catlin of the "Use Your Inside Voice" blog makes a few suggestions for the introverted manager looking to utilize the natural strengths of extroverts. In addition to some of the more stereotypical uses of extroverted sociability like planning social events and introducing colleagues at social functions, Catlin also suggests deputizing your extroverted staff members to organize recognition initiatives for the office, as well as creating "hang-out" time during all-day meetings or off-campus meetings.

Storytelling Through Staff Meetings

> In recent years, social scientists have come to appreciate what political, religious, and military figures have long known: that stories (narratives, myths, or fables) constitute a uniquely powerful currency in human relationships. -Howard Gardner, *Leading Minds*

Introverts are fascinated with stories. Connections

between seemingly disparate bits of information are necessary in order for the world to make sense, and what better way to relate information than with a story? A 1956 study by cognitive psychologist George Miller revealed that the average human mind can hold roughly seven chunks of knowledge at any given time. While the extroverted mind is better equipped to move seamlessly between those seven units, introverts have an easier time comprehending that information if it can be connected.

As I became familiar with Miller and his study, I suddenly had a greater understanding of and appreciation for one of my favorite pastimes- reading. Books (or articles, or plays, or anything else I would read) are collections of interconnected facts, dialogue and ideas- stories. Even with nonfictional works or textbooks that are designed to inform rather than entertain, they have a comfortable cadence and predictability. What's more, the information given within them is easier to digest for its sequential nature.

But my next thought as I pondered the impact of Miller's work was how it affects me in less comfortable arenas. The first applicable scenario that came to mind: **staff meetings**. Staff meetings, if conducted as most are, can be hell on earth for introverts. Agendas shift quickly from one topic to the next, a problem often exacerbated by imposed time limits. "Report-outs" are common, with the progress of departments or divisions occasionally requiring an on-the-spot reaction to information. Generally speaking, the staff meeting can be a particularly prickly, but unavoidable, part of the workweek. As the recently appointed chair of a committee that meets biweekly with constituents from the six colleges of our consortium, I've tried to lead these meetings with respect for the time of others, while at the same time respecting my own nature and that of other introverts in the group.

Is it possible to structure staff meetings in the same way that an author crafts a novel or a reporter crafts an article? I know of many an introvert that would appreciate that. What could that look like?

Meeting organizers, if you will be working with an agenda, send it out in advance. My agendas draw liberally from the minutes of the previous meeting, but also include cartoons or funny pictures to show my sense of humor about the work we do. Familiarity with what issues will be discussed and what questions will be asked could help reduce the disorientation that comes with spontaneous lines of questioning; the personal touch provides a reminder that you recognize the humanity of the people you're working with. What's more, meetings can move more quickly if people are able to plan their responses. If you are not an agenda user, even a quick overview of what questions might be raised during the meeting could suffice. Returning for just a moment to the quick operational definition of introversion ("easily overstimulated"), the preparation phase for a meeting can help mitigate that potential shock that comes with an unanticipated query.

Consider a preamble or foreword to the meeting. Any information that may need to be known in advance of discussion (changing climate for a decision, factors to consider when assigning tasks) should be provided at the outset of the meeting. Some may argue that the information could be sent out over email; in some cases that could be appropriate. However, when the background information is sensitive to tone, electronic communication may need to be eschewed in favor of a more expressive medium.

Another literary technique that could make meetings a less daunting endeavor for all involved is foreshadowing. By creating opportunities for a meeting or project's purpose to be fully realized, some content may need to be generated in advance. Marla Gottschalk of The Office Blend understands the importance of letting introverts generate ideas and "hints" to later action prior to the main event:

> It would be misguided to expect an opinion from an introvert at the drop of a hat [...] if you offer an introvert a period of time to process you'll likely take full advantage of their vantage point and skill set [...] Be sure to offer opportunities for introverts to start the idea generation process before team meetings and allow points in the conversation where they can jump in.

This foreshadowing technique will allow introverts to come to a meeting with more fully formed ideas, greater confidence in their opinions, and a heightened ability to address any questions that may arise about what they're bringing to the group.

Other tips for running "introvert-friendly meetings" as a manager:

> **Try to structure the meeting in such a way that the flow of information is logical.** Here again, the shift from one item to the next can be difficult to wrap one's head around, for introverts and extroverts alike. Even if disjointed topics can't be arranged thematically, consider a chronological or priority based arrangement of agenda items. If the system can be understood, this can help an introvert be more present during these gatherings.

> **Give these meetings the time they truly deserve.** Too often, staff meetings discourage dialogue where it may be needed, for the sake of time. But it should be noted that in sacrificing length of conversation, rushed staff meetings could also cheat introverts out of an opportunity to contribute. To communicate well, time is needed to process information, but *also* to craft our responses. Make sure the efficient structure of your meeting isn't at the expense of a rich,

meaningful and necessary discussion.

End the meeting with a review of action steps. Much like a dissertation or other scholarly publication concludes with implications and next steps, meetings can as well. After a period where information has been fed in a steady stream, the clarity that can come from a quick summary or explicit voicing of action steps is invaluable- I would imagine that even extroverts would appreciate that summation of the meeting's events.

Recognition of Introverts

As I continue my discussion on managing introverts, I would be remiss if I failed to address the topic of recognition. For managers who aim to properly recognize their staff members, the default response (even for introverted managers) is to shower them with praise, ideally in a public fashion, ensuring that all can recognize their good works. While I would hesitate to say that *no* introvert would appreciate being recognized in such a manner, I would say that this is often difficult for introverts to handle. The concentrated spotlight, combined with little warning on how to conduct oneself, is a wonderful recipe for the overstimulated environment that could cause an introvert to shut down.

On the other hand, many introverts' default internalization methods mean that they are quicker to see the flaws in their work than the gems. When they do good work, they may not admit to needing to hear it. But they truly do.

How do you walk the line between embarrassing a high-achieving introvert and ignoring his or her good work to preserve comfort? Gottschalk offers one potential way to mitigate the shock that comes with an unexpected honor, cautioning, "[I]f they are about to receive an award or accolade, let them know what you're planning ahead of time. They'll appreciate the gesture and have time to prepare." Will it spoil the surprise? Well, sure. But the discomfort surrounding such an unexpected shower of attention and stimulation would ruin it too. Another technique that you could employ? Making your commendations in writing. Be it a thoughtful and heartfelt greeting card recognizing the staff member's contribution, or a more public display via a widely distributed email or departmental newsletter, it commends the exemplary individual in question without bestowing energy-sapping attention upon him or her. This attention to not just the achievements of the person, but also his or her preference for recognition, could make the difference between a great boss, and a horrible one.

It has been said that when people leave organizations, they are actually leaving managers. Although countless factors can contribute to an individual leaving his or her manager, feeling understood is a desire we all have in the workplace and beyond. By taking time to understand introverted staff members, find out their needs and wishes for a comfortable and effective work environment, and respect their way of working, you may not completely win over any employee; it is, however, a wonderful start that will be much appreciated.

INsights

⇒ Do you make time at the start of an

employee's time with you to identify how they work, how they like to be recognized, and what they need to be successful? Making time for that could help all employees, and is particularly helpful for introverts.

⇒ When planning meetings, make sure to start promptly and be considerate of time. Include agendas ahead of time if possible, or otherwise strive to keep meetings focused.

⇒ If you are supervising introverts, don't assume that you can "set them and forget them," so to speak. They will still want face time, so strive to check in with them periodically and see how they're doing.

⇒ Make the opportunity to follow up after meetings, evaluations, or projects well known, and acceptable in multiple forms. It may be easier for them to submit testimony in writing, so allow for that when collecting feedback.

CONCLUSION

In *Helping College Students*, Marcia Roe Clark recognizes the human capital necessary to be successful in the field of student affairs, acknowledging the impact we can have on students when we commit to doing our best work:

> Student affairs administrators are among the most prominent helpers on many college and university campuses [...] professionals are employed in positions with high levels of student contact, providing direct service to students in the form of facilitating, advising, problem solving, mentoring, supervising, and

training.

She goes on to list several of the competencies that are helpful in achieving success in our varied roles, using a 2005 study from Burkhard, et al as a guide:

> Reflecting a consensus of a hundred-plus mid- and senior level administrators, the researchers identified human relations skills and personal qualities as the two most important competency areas for entry-level professionals, noting that these skills span across functional areas as diverse as admissions, residence life, athletics, and academic services. Human relations skills include competencies such as collaboration, active listening, and multicultural competency. In contrast, confrontation, oral communication, and interpersonal relations were among the competencies categorizes as personal qualities, or "unique individual characteristics"

Roe quickly points out that these skills span across functional areas in the field; I would like to make the point that they span across temperamental tendencies as well. None of the aforementioned skills, ones deemed essential by rising and current leaders in our field, are exclusive to extroverts. As my friend Ryan mentioned in the introduction, anyone who is called to do this work can do it well. However, it is not equally easy for all who choose to undertake it.

You may recall my definition of "masking introversion" from Chapter Four: masking introversion is not faking the ability to be social without bounds; it is the appearance that such behavior is easy. Sometimes the breadth of the aforementioned expectations can cause you to feel overwhelmed or overstimulated. Sometimes the trademark introvert focus can induce weariness when "left on" for too long. But the need to slow down, step away, and recharge should not be considered a weakness. It should be seen as a necessary element of ensuring our own strength. Robert B. Young's "Philosophies and Values Guiding the Student Affairs Profession" cites caring as a significant element in doing successful, meaningful work in our profession. The ability to care is not confined to any one temperament. So long as the professional is willing to apply an attitude of care to the work that we do, temperament is of little consequence. Introverts, be confident in the gifts and qualities that make you who you are. Your deliberate and contemplative leadership is needed to take this field into the future. Though it may not always be easy, and it may not always seem as though it will be worth it, this field needs you and your gifts. The I's, truly do, have it.

ACKNOWLEDGEMENTS

Oh, man. This part makes me more than a little nervous. I don't want to forget anyone, and—in true introvert/Canadian fashion—I worry deeply about the offense that such an omission would cause. So here we go. Sorry in advance.

Lots of people in my life have told me, "You should write a book!" This is either (a) a tribute to you all, or (b) your fault. Let me know which you decide on!

I also have a lot of friends who were kind enough to jump on the board with me writing for lots and lots of consecutive pages, even when I wasn't fully confident in the idea. The question, "How's the book coming?" is a terrifying and powerful one; when you get asked enough times, things start to come together. To my friends, colleagues, and strongest supporters- I am better for knowing you. I'll now attempt to name you in reverse alphabetical order: Valerie Heruska, Shannon Hubert, Mallory Bower, Laurie Berry, Laura McClernon, Joel Pettigrew, Joe Ginese, Jeff Parker, Jeff Lail, Jason Meier, Eric Stoller, Elia Ajram, Chris Conzen, Becca Obergefell, Ann Marie Klotz, Amanda Glover, and Adam Dangelo.

And in a paragraph of her own, because she is in a class of her own, I want to thank the illustrator of this book, Sue Caulfield. Not only has Sue tirelessly and unwaveringly encouraged me through the writing process, but she allowed me to borrow her talents to illustrate key points. It is an honor to be able to feature her "Sue-dles" in this volume. She is an artist who has an amazing ability to help others around them believe they're also creating art, and I am immeasurably thankful for that.

I will share a public thank you to two famous authors introverts who were kind enough to indulge me in conversation about this area of interest. To Susan Cain and Adam Grant, your work has made me an exponentially better professional, writer, and person. Thank you, thank you, thank you.

This isn't just my story. I set out with the intention of incorporating the experiences of several other individuals to ensure that it wasn't just my story. And I am so thankful to those who let me share a bit of their lives in these pages. The default internalization that introverts are so prone to make us feel like we're alone sometimes. I am indebted to you all for proving that voice in my head wrong. Here again, in reverse alphabetical order: Ryan Manning, Monica Fochtman, Lisa Endersby, Kelley Stier, Julia Fleming, Joanna Garcia, Jessica Philo, Jessi Robinson, Jeff Pelletier, Jeff Parker, Jason Meier, Heidi Thuessen, Emily Mire, Debra Sanborn, Dana McNulty, Curtis Tarver, and Cassidy Sansone.

Above all, I have to recognize my family. To my sister Nana, who can drop some wildly insightful wisdom given her relative young age, thank you for helping me push through to finish this thing when I wasn't sure I could. To my parents Kofi and Rose, who funded what I'm sure was an insanely expensive book habit, I am thankful to you for giving me enough exposure to good writing to recognize when mine needed some work. All that I am—appreciative of hard work, respectful, curious, and constantly striving to learn more—I owe to you.

ON THE SHOULDERS OF GIANTS

References and Guides for Further Reading

Resources listed in this section have either been quoted directly, or in some way inspired the direction that this volume took. There's a great deal of information out there on this topic, and I would strongly encourage you to continue exploring the literature if you're so inclined!

Books
200 Best Jobs for Introverts, compiled by Jist's Best Jobs

Confessions of an Introvert: The Shy Girl's Guide to Career, Networking,
    and Getting the Most Out of Life by Meghan Wier
Give and Take by Adam Grant
Helping College Students: Developing Essential Support Skills for Student
    Affairs Practice, edited by Amy L. Reynolds
Introvert Power by Laurie Helgoe
Introverts in the Church by Adam McHugh
Leading Minds: An Anatomy of Leadership by Howard Gardner
Lincoln on Leadership by Donald T. Phillips
Quiet by Susan Cain
Student Services: A Handbook for the Profession, edited by Susan Komives
    and Dudley B. Woodard, Jr.
The Cult of Personality Testing: How Personality Tests are Leading Us To
    Miseducate Our Children, Mismanage Our Companies, and
    Misunderstand Ourselves by Annie Murphy Paul
The Hidden Gifts of the Introverted Child by Marti Olson Laney
The Introvert Advantage by Marti Olson Laney

The Introvert and Extrovert in Love: Making Love Work When Opposites
 Attract by Marti Olson Laney
The Introvert's Way: Living a Quiet Life in a Noisy World by Sophia Dembling

Articles
Academy of Management Journal: Reversing the Extraverted Leadership
 Advantage: The Role of Employee Productivity by Adam Grant, Francesca Gino and David Hoffman
Association for Supervision and Curriculum Development: Introverts and
 Extroverts Require Different Learning Environments by Ronald R. Schmeck and Dan Lockhart
Education Weekly: Studies Illustrate Plight of Introverted Students by Sarah
 Sparks
Edutopia: Introversion and the Invisible Adolescent by Mark Phillips
Edutopia: Embracing Introversion: Ways to Stimulate Reserved Students in
 the Classroom by Tony Baldasaro
Faith on Campus: Unlikely Student Leaders(?)- The

Introverts by Guy Chmieleski

GSU Master Teaching Program: On Learning Styles by Harvey Brightman

LinkedIn/The Office Blend: A Note About Introverts and Teams by Marla Gottschalk

LinkedIn/The Office Blend: How Not to Manage an Introvert by Marla Gottschalk

Quiet: The Missing Chapter by Karen Catlin

Scientific Learning: Introverted Students in the Classroom: Nurturing Their Hidden Strengths by Sherelle Walker

The Chronicle of Higher Education: Screening Out the Introverts by William Pannapacker

Workopolis: The Unspoken Leaders: Why It's Time for Introverts to Take Charge by Nicole Wray

Workplace Mojo: 8 Advantages of Introverts by Matt Monge

BONUS RESOURCE:
Guide for Interviewing the Introvert

Statistics tell us that somewhere between 1/3 and 1/2 of the population in the US in introverted; this percentage is highly likely to apply to our pool of student leader candidates. From resident assistants to orientation leaders, admissions ambassadors to student desk workers, all of the students we educate are capable of greatness.

As evaluators of their talent and potential, it is imperative that we know what to look for; moreover, we must try to understand the many different types of student leader we could encounter. Consider the tips below as you work with and observe students throughout the selection process:

1) **Temper the atmosphere of the room to create comfort.** In baking, to "temper" a substance such as eggs or chocolate is to bring down the temperature gradually to prevent it from breaking or cooking too quickly. Sometimes students, particularly those who are new to the interview

process, need us to temper the interview situation to allow them to be the best versions of themselves. This includes introducing yourself warmly, welcoming them to the room, and letting them know that the interview is a conversation. With that said, this should not be an invitation to not take the interview seriously. We need to know that these students are capable of being professional, and an interview is the first place we'll likely get to see that competency from them. Strive to create an unintimidating, but professional, environment.

2) **Patiently allow time for the interviewee to respond.** Even for the most prepared students, a response to a direct question doesn't always come quickly. Let the candidate know at the outset that it's okay to take a moment to think about a question before responding, and hold true to that promise. Make sure that your nonverbal cues match this voiced patience- if candidates feel you are getting impatient, it could affect their performance.

3) **Weigh written responses, performance in the group, and individual encounters with equal reverence.** A hallmark of the introverted mind is a heightened performance when given time to think or reflect, a difference that shows up when comparing written responses to in-person performance. Of course, I would never advocate for a student who was qualified on paper but legitimately couldn't perform in a flexible, spontaneous environment. But I would encourage you to look for understanding of the job responsibilities in person and on paper.

4) **Consider expanding or redefining the "look" of a student leader.** It is easy to pick the most visible, loudest, or most self-assured student leaders. But I would challenge you to consider the diversity of our incoming students. Some of them will come in with a clear idea of what they want from their experience. Others will not, and may need to be talked to closely or listened to about their aspirations. Introverts excel at this. Create space on the team for those students who aren't always the loudest, and create space in

your notion of a student leader for those who sit back a little longer before they shout. Chances are they will have some great things to say when they eventually speak up.

Made in the USA
Lexington, KY
12 March 2017